LIFE AFTER CHILD LOSS

THE MOTHER'S SURVIVAL GUIDE TO COPE AND FIND JOY

PEGGY GREEN

Difference Press

Washington, DC, USA

Published 2020

Cover Design: Jennifer Stimson

Editing: Cory Hott

Author Photo Credit: Donna Sweetin, Sweetin Photography

PRAISE FOR PEGGY GREEN

"*Life after Child Loss* is both an insightful guide and knowledgeable resource. Peggy Green offers unique wisdom and useful steps to help you find your way on your grief path. As a mother who is also walking the path of child loss after the sudden and unexpected passing of my son, Thomas, in 2018, this book has brought me much needed hope and a deeper understanding of how to not only survive child loss, but to also thrive."

— JESS GREISE, MOTHER

"Peggy Green has created an inspirational and accessible guidebook to support parents following the death of a child. Her experience with loss allows her permission to touch the most intimate and fragile parts of your heart and mind. Whether on a new journey or still struggling years later, *Life after Child Loss* is a welcome gift for those seeking growth and recovery."

— RENEE EAKINS, RETIRED HIGH SCHOOL ENGLISH TEACHER

"In *Life after Child Loss*, Peggy Green details her ongoing journey of life, love, and loss. Through the immeasurable fog of grief, Peggy has reached deep to lend a warm heart and hand to those who are fellow loss travelers. The strategies and insights she outlined will be a road map and lifeline to many as they navigate uncharted waters."

— DONNA SWEETIN, PHOTOGRAPHER

"*Life after Child Loss* will speak directly to your heart. The title says it all. It is exceedingly rare to find someone so honest and caring, and have them relay their feelings and emotions like Peggy does. There are a lot of helpful insights and steps to guide you through the trauma of losing a child."

— DIANA BENNETT, MOTHER

"*Life after Child Loss* gives you permission, and teaches you to give yourself permission, to process your loss and provides strategies to keep taking steps on your journey. Having never been through this process before, this book was educational and enlightening in so many ways. The education for building a framework of support is instrumental in everyone's health, no matter what life struggle you are working through. Peggy speaks her truth with a raw honesty while showing you real, actionable techniques and options. Start at the beginning or jump in the middle. You will find hope, solace, and real solutions."

— KATHY PARADES, BUSINESS OWNER

"*Life after Child Loss* feels like Peggy is right there cheering you on. In actuality, she has done exactly that for me, even in the midst of her pain. As a living example of her framework of tools, she has encouraged me to choose personal growth over staying stuck in hard, unpleasant emotions by taking action. This also relates to how I love the way Peggy teaches about choices as a theme. Throughout her framework, she illustrates how it begins with an intentional mindset that drives actions when using the tools. "

— HOLLY FERGUSON, RETIRED PHYSICAL EDUCATOR AND DENTAL HYGIENIST

"In *Life after Child Loss,* Peggy Green takes her darkest times and turns them into a beacon of hope for other loss travelers. A must-read for anyone ready to begin their journey toward finding joy after loss. "

— LISA CAIRE, MOTHER

"Ms. Green has 'been there and done that." Twice. She knows that grief is unique to each individual dealing with the loss of a loved one. Personally, knowing how death hurts, and now having read Ms. Green's heartfelt and compassionately written *Life after Child Loss,* I wish I had had her book for support after my husband passed away. I sincerely recommend this book to anyone having to deal with this life situation. "

— JF RIDGLEY, AUTHOR OF *RED FURY REVOLT*

"*Life after Child Loss* belongs in the hands of anyone dealing with loss of a loved one. I have witnessed Peggy's journey and transformation of grief over time. She walks the talk and has implemented these techniques into her life. As well as offering hope and strength to other parents experiencing grief of losing a child, my mom's optimism and light can be felt in these pages. I hope her framework and steps laid out here can help heal your broken heart as it did for me."

— BRITTANY GREEN, DAUGHTER AND MOTHER

"In *Life after Child Loss: The Mother's Survival Guide to Cope and Find Joy,* my mom consolidated the advice she has ingrained in me into one place. I have no doubt many others will benefit from the tools outlined and feel more confident in their healing journey."

— HANNAH GREEN, DAUGHTER AND STUDENT

CONTENTS

For my son Connor. If it weren't for you taking your life by suicide, I would not have written this book. You told me that you weren't done on earth, and the only way to help others would be through me. I love you to the stars and back.

FOREWORD

I first met Peggy Green several years ago while caring for her mother who was on hospice. While I knew she would experience the loss of her mother, I had no idea that years later she would be helping others by writing this book after surviving the loss of two children. I still remember many months after her mother died when she called me to be put in touch with the bereavement chaplain. She had been doing very well with her grief, however that day she needed to put her cat down. This opened up a flood of emotions and she needed a little extra support.

After reading *Life after Child Loss*, I see that she has not only been in the place where you are now, but she has also developed a framework that will allow you to choose what techniques are right for you so you can move at your pace through your own grief journey. As Peggy has proven, you, too, can achieve joy again, become stronger mentally and physically, and develop a deep gratitude for what is still present in your life.

As a hospice medical director, I have attended many lectures and seminars and read a wide array of books on the subject of grief and loss. Peggy provides such a unique perspective of this journey and can give you advice and techniques that come not from the classroom, but from her real-life experiences.

Many people are familiar with the five stages of grief put forward by Elizabeth Kubler- Ross in her book "On death and dying." While not everyone experiences all five stages or follows them in a predictive pattern it does serve as a framework to help understand the emotions of someone who is terminally ill or those that have lost a loved one.

In *Life After Child Loss,* Peggy provides a framework to allow you, the reader, to accept and deal with loss, and ultimately move forward to regain joy in your life.

As you progress on your grief journey, you do not have to utilize all of the tools in this framework; rather choose the ones that are right for you and begin. You'll likely come back to this framework again and again as your outlook changes and you find yourself in different places with different needs over time.

This book is important because it addresses not only the psychological aspect of loss, but includes the spiritual aspect and physical well-being of the reader. This is similar to what Cicely Saunders referred to as "total pain," and is the foundation upon which the hospice philosophy of care is based.

While I, personally and professionally, have also dealt with loss, I thankfully have never had to deal with what you and Peggy have gone through the loss of a child. But it happened, and here you are. Use this book as one of your many support tools. Start to journal, find your tribe, and utilize whatever advice on these pages speaks to you. And like Peggy, hopefully you, too, will begin to regain your joy.

Robert Howe, DO
Medical Director, Compassus Hospice

1

RADICAL ACCEPTANCE OF THE LOSS OF YOUR CHILD

You suffered a loss, the loss of a child. It is a terrible place to be. I am so sorry that you are here. I am sorry that you are going through this. Your child may have recently passed away or it may have been years ago. The loss of a child is as deep as it gets. Grief is deep and aching when they are no longer with us. You may feel there is no consolation, not even believing that you will see them again removes the pain that your child is gone. I understand. I have been through all of this and more. Let me paint you a picture.

You will never get over your loss. You move through it. Outsiders have the expectation you will return to the way you were before this all happened, that you should easily move on in life and there is a time limit on your grief.

Moving through loss is recognizing and accepting that your child is gone. You give yourself grace in feeling your emotions, pain, and heartache. It is being able to be happy and joyful without feeling guilty. It is giving yourself permission to remember your child, love them, and look toward a future. Your pain never totally goes away. It lessens, but is always with you. That is moving through child loss.

These may be some of the emotions you are or will be feeling.

Initially you experienced numbness and lack of feeling. This is your mind's way of shielding you from the pain.

Then came the anger. Perhaps you expressed it toward God, other people, or the circumstances. When your world has come to a complete halt, how can the world keep spinning? It is just not fair.

It is all a bad dream. You still expect your child to fly through the door or you will hear their cry. You might be trying to make sense of what happened. Your thinking may be clouded; you may find it difficult to focus. Maybe you're questioning your sanity.

As a grieving parent, you may want to say "I love you" one more time, kiss their cheek, or have one more hug. You become consumed with guilt. What could you have done differently to prevent this from happening? You punish yourself and deny yourself the right to ever feel joy again.

Dreams that belong to you as a parent have been ripped out of your hands. The hope to see milestones in their lives: walking, graduations, weddings, and grandchildren.

Grief impacts us in so many ways and can take over all parts of our lives. This is why I decided to share my own journey as a loss traveler and equip others with the tools to help move through the loss of your child and guide you toward being happy again.

RADICAL ACCEPTANCE

I recently listened to a podcast, *Oprah's SuperSoul Conversations*, with Oprah Winfrey interviewing Lady Gaga.

Gaga shared some deep and personal stories about her health struggles and childhood trauma. She shared that at nineteen years old she was raped, and experiences lingering PTSD. She has been in chronic pain from head to toe with fibromyalgia, been a cutter, and has other mental health challenges. I was impressed with her honesty and vulnerability. It hit me square in the eyes. I immediately knew this applied to the grief process.

> *"Radical acceptance applies to every crisis, every difficulty, every challenge in your life. Stress comes from wanting something to be what it isn't and doesn't change until you first accept it for what is, then make a decision as to 'what do I do next.'"*
>
> — OPRAH WINFREY

You may be asking yourself how does this apply to your grief. Allow me to explain. I wish I could magically bring your child back to life. The reality is that no matter what I do, no matter how hard I pray, beg, or plead, your child is gone. Accepting they are gone is the first step to move forward in your process. You are accepting your child left their earthly body. However, you may not know what to do next.

That is why you are here. You want to move through the loss and reclaim hope and your happiness again. I assume you have not experienced the death of a child before and this is all new to you. How to handle grief is not in a handbook that floods from the heavens. We learn how to move through it from experience, just like on-the-job training. Moving through your loss does not just happen. I can promise that it will take a conscious decision to heal. Your brain, heart, and body have experienced trauma, just like your body does when you fall and break a bone. If you leave the bone to heal on itself, you may wind up with a misshapen arm or leg, one that you can't use to pick up a grocery bag or walk.

GRIEF'S IMPACT

Grief, when not processed, can and most likely will come out in what I call "sideways." What I mean by that is that your relationships may fail due to uncontrolled anger. You may lose your job because your depression keeps you from going to work. Lack of income may lead to loss of housing. Anxiety and depression inhibit sleep which aids in the healing process from trauma. There may be health consequences that lead to heart attack, stroke, obesity, diabetes, and much more. These things may not immediately surface. It may take years. Over time anger, shock, confusion, and guilt can build up and implode your life.

There are multiple physical symptoms of grief. Be in tune with your body. Is it telling you something? Are you feeling things differently that weren't present before this happened? This is not an all-inclusive list. You may be experiencing others.

Do you feel fatigued and exhausted all the time? Are you constantly ready for a nap? After sleeping for the night, do you still feel tired?

Do you have more aches and pains than usual? Do you feel like you have the flu that just won't go away? Grief can exacerbate pain.

Are you having more headaches? Stress contributes to headaches and you are in a stressful season.

Are you losing your keys and cell phone or don't remember what you were saying? This is common due to competing thoughts.

Do you have difficulty eating? Are you binging on sugary sweets? Is your stomach upset?

Have you had more colds, coughs, fevers? With stress comes a weakened immune system.

Do you have difficulty breathing? The emotion of grief is associated with lung function. It constrains the lungs and the ability to move.

My wish for you is that you take a different path and I am so glad you made the choice to be here.

IT'S ALL ABOUT CHOICES

I am a major believer in choices and self-responsibility. What we think, how we act, and how we respond to life is totally up to us. I don't blame anyone for my choices. This concept may be a bit difficult to digest right now, so allow me to explain. All of us go through tough circumstances. Believe me, I've had more than my fair share. I could sit and wallow in self-pity or decide to make the most of the circumstances which have been handed to me. I am not happy about what has happened. There are some things I just can't change.

Radical acceptance. I do like the principle. It makes sense in my ever-changing world. I've accepted what has happened. It is the next step of making a choice with what I have been handed. I choose to love life. I choose to process my grief. I choose to live in the moment and not try to re-create what can't be re-created. You too have a choice to love life now. You have a new norm. It is a dark and heart-wrenching place. You never asked to be in this place, part of this grieving parents club. I get it. It is difficult.

May you find comfort in knowing you are not alone on this journey; other parents have gone through the same thing. They have survived. They have found joy. They live without guilt. What you decide to do with your new norm is up to you.

One of the biggest fears of a parent after their loss is that their child will be forgotten. In your attempt to hold onto your memories, you may be reluctant to step out of the darkness. Your child will not be forgotten. In the beginning, it may be difficult to think about your child without buckets of tears. That is normal. Tears are healing. They help to express your emotions. Looking at pictures of your child can help you move through your grief. Memories cannot be taken away. Those memories will help you to heal. Hold onto them tightly. But this does not mean you need to stay in the darkness.

It is easy to see only darkness with the loss of a child. It is a natural reaction. In times of trouble it is difficult to be grateful on any level. I totally understand if you find it difficult to be grateful for anything at this point in your life. One of the things I do is write what I am grateful for on a small sticky note and place it in a gratitude jar. Examples of my gratitude are simple. I am grateful for my warm bed. I am grateful for the sunshine. I am grateful for a hot shower. I am grateful that I am healthy. I am grateful for spring. That simple act of acknowledging good things helps to turn my thinking from desperation to joy. It works. It works in our subconscious mind. It tells our conscious brain to see the good things even in difficult circumstances.

Above all, be gentle with yourself and let yourself grieve. I am still in the process and have cried in the grocery store, on the phone, and at the gym. Give yourself permission to be happy. Lose the guilt over happiness. Your child wants you to move forward. This experience has changed you. There is no going back. Be open to the new chapter in your life. It can either be written without your approval or you can take charge of what you do.

GRIEF ON YOUR TERMS

As loss travelers, we learn that grief is individualized. We learn that you can grieve on your terms. I've survived the losses of two children. Most recently it was my twenty-four-year-old son who passed away. Upon the breaking news of his death, I had dozens of people tell me what I should be doing and how to grieve. I was flooded with text messages, emails, and Facebook messages on what books to read, what groups to attend, and what to believe. I was so touched by the outpouring of caring and love, yet at the same time overwhelmed. I sincerely thanked each person who offered advice.

I kept their recommendations in a folder "for later." That later for the need if I ever wanted it. What upset me, though, was several people were offended when I told them I was not ready for their suggestions. I even had one friend become indignant with me and insist that I follow her advice. I politely told her that I wasn't ready and that if the time came, I would check it out. Not only was I dealing with the loss of a child but was now being told how to grieve for him. This was a double whammy that I didn't want to deal with.

Nevertheless, I know every single one of those friends were well-intentioned and it came from their heartfelt desire to help. It was then that I decided that my grief journey would be on my terms, my way, and with what worked for me. With that being said, I am offering the framework for what worked for me. It does not have to be yours. Nothing is being imposed on you. You came here looking for help and that is precisely what I wish for you. But you choose. You can choose to take it all, take a little, or none of it at all. Most importantly, all the experiences, tools, and insights I share in this book are meant to support you so that you move through your loss and give yourself permission to be happy again.

2

THE CHILD LOSS CLUB

The subject of losing a child is unfathomable. I belong to a club that I never asked to join. I was forced into it. Blindsided and left to fend for myself. No one else I knew was in this club. It seemed an exclusive club. And people were not clamoring to get into it. This club is called "child loss." There is darkness to this club that outsiders do not want to talk about. However, I, Peggy Green, do want to talk about it.

PHONE CALL NUMBER ONE

My daughter Courtney was only nine months old when she died. It was a horrible accident. The morning she died it was her dad Jesse's day to take her to daycare. She cried when I left. I gave her a big hug and put her back in her crib. We had talked about how much Courtney was starting to scooch across the floor. In no time she would be rolling around, then walking. She was a beautiful ball of joy. Her hair was a fuzzy blond and looked so much like her Grandpa Green. She loved to go on walks in her stroller and be outdoors.

I received a call at work that something was wrong with her and I needed to get to the hospital as soon as possible. This was before cell phones. I called my parents and asked them to meet me at the hospital because I couldn't get in touch with Jesse. It was rush hour. The police insisted I have a coworker drive me. He drove like a mad man to get me there. He snuck through lines at stoplights, went down the side of the highway, and drove over the speed limit. After what seemed hours, we pulled into the emergency room driveway.

As we pulled up, I saw my dad and another man waiting for us. As soon as I got out of the car and came close enough to the man, I saw his name tag. It said Chaplain. It was then I knew Courtney was dead. Dad confirmed my biggest fear. Courtney was dead. I was ushered into a room where my mom sat. She was in tears as I ran to her. The three of us, Mom, Dad, and I, hugged. It was horrible. My head was spinning. How? She was at the babysitter's? The babysitter loved Courtney.

I still hadn't managed to reach Jesse at that point. He was working as a salesman and not in the office. It was his night to pick Courtney up from the sitter. I frantically called all his buddies to see if they knew where he was. No one knew. One was even joking with me and in my desperation to find Jesse, I yelled, "Courtney is dead. Where is Jesse?" I'm known for being pretty direct and this got the point across. While I was tracking Jesse down, the police were at the sitter's house. They were waiting for Jesse to pick up Courtney. When he showed up, they directed him to the hospital. We met at the hospital in that tiny room with family members who gathered.

I asked to see Courtney. I was told it would not be pretty. I didn't care. I had to. I had to make it real. It was ugly. Her tiny body lying on the table. It was cold. It was sterile. In my grief and desperation, I yelled at her, "Courtney, wake up!" I knew it wasn't going to happen, but we do crazy things in grief. Unbeknownst to me, this would not be the first of many insane thoughts or actions. Grief does weird things to the way we think and act.

PHONE CALL NUMBER TWO

Connor is my only son. At twenty-four years old, he was growing into a fine young man. He was patient and kind. He was the kind of guy who would do anything to help someone else, even to his detriment. Connor would help others move, risking being late for work because his friends were more important.

After Connor got sober, he became fully involved in the twelve-step program. One of the basic tenets of recovery groups is to give back by volunteering. Without money management experience, he volunteered as the treasurer for one of his weekly meetings. He felt an obligation to give back to the community which helped him in his sobriety. He also gave back by sponsoring his peers to help them work through their program. He was a teacher and a friend.

He loved dogs and rescued Mac. He is a beautiful mix of Labrador, pit bull and St. Bernard. Imagine big, playful, and stubborn. Mac had terrible behavior. I remember encouraging Connor to take Mac back. He was too much work, too hard to handle. Connor had none of it. He took it upon himself to train Mac. Through time and effort, Mac became a well-behaved companion. He loved walks, playing with other dogs, and lying next to Connor as he played games on Xbox.

My son was a good kid. He made some mistakes in his life but nothing that couldn't be fixed. Connor loved to skateboard. He received a skateboard for Christmas when he was around nine years old. Once that got in his hands, or he got his feet on it, there was no stopping him. He learned to "do stairs," flip his board, ride ramps, and ride the rails. I remember watching him teach a young boy at the skate park. He showed patience with others. He had no fear. He wasn't afraid of getting hurt. He had a heart for others.

Connor loved his family. We shared the love of dogs, hiking, and the mountains. We also talked about business, and that it was about making a customer happy and helping them realize their dreams. We talked the same language.

Connor took responsibility for his actions. He knew his decisions were his. He was that young man who didn't blame anyone for his life circumstances.

On December 14, 2018 in the midst of rush-hour traffic. I answered a phone call from a number I did not recognize. It was my oldest daughter, Brittany. She said, "Mom." Then I heard her say to another person, "I know he hasn't been feeling well." My gut told me to get off the highway if I needed to turn around. Then nothing. She didn't respond to me when I called out her name. By now my stomach was flipping. I knew she was talking about her brother, my son, Connor. They worked together at car dealerships next to each other. It was common that they were together, helping each other. I hung up and called her back on her private cell phone. It was then Brittany told me, "Mom, I don't know how to tell you this, but Connor is dead. He killed himself." My heart stopped. I shouted out at the top of my lungs: "*Nooooo!*" How could this be? Connor, my only son. Dead? Why? How? All the questions came flooding in.

I immediately got back on the highway and called a friend. She told me to come pick her up and she would go with me to see my son. I was shaking. I was in tears. I was crying out to God. Why? Why? Why?

What happened next is all a blur.

I don't remember who else I called. I picked up my friend

and it was an excruciating ride in bumper to bumper traffic to get across town to see my son, my daughters, and my niece, Mickey. My youngest daughter, Hannah, was on that side of town and beat me to the dealership. My niece's business is on that side of town. She beat me there. Connor's dad even beat me there.

When we got there, I ran in to hug my girls. I vaguely remember shouting "No. No. No. Why? Why? Why? How can this be?" The police were already there. They had started their investigation. After what seemed like forever, we were asked if we wanted to see Connor. Yes, I had to. I felt that if I didn't see him, it wouldn't be real. It was all a bad dream. I said yes. Brittany, my friend, and I went around the corner to see him. He looked as if he was asleep. I knelt beside him and just looked at him. I was afraid to touch him. I felt Brittany's eyes on the back of my head. I met my friend's eyes as I knelt next to my son. Her eyes were filled with tears and compassion. I felt the police officers watching me. I was afraid they would yell at me. It was now a crime scene. Even though it was evident it was suicide, they needed to confirm no foul play. An autopsy had to be completed. Connor had to be taken to the police morgue. We weren't leaving until he was picked up. Those hours were the longest of my life, waiting and waiting. I watched in shock as my son was taken away on a gurney in a black body bag. It was surreal. It was like the movies. However, this time, it was not an empty bag filled to look like a human, it was my son. I couldn't believe this was happening.

FAMILY LOSSES

My father, the one who met me at the hospital when Courtney died, passed away in 1999. He was only sixty-nine years old. He was my mentor. He was the one who taught me to have goals. He taught me to take care of myself. He taught me how to wire a ceiling light. He taught me about finances. He taught me to garden and love the outdoors. He was that positive male figure. I read *Catcher in the Rye* out loud to him in his final week. We always talked about reading it together but never got around to it. I read it. He listened. I know he heard me even though he couldn't tell me. It was that last father-daughter thing we did together.

My father passed away from colon cancer. His cancer surfaced after an extremely stressful time in his life. It was about his relationship with his father. His dad disowned him and removed him from his will, all because of a small disagreement that blew out of proportion. It was horrible and I know Dad was ruined. The rest of the family was devastated. Dad wasn't one to express his emotions, but I knew he was disappointed about the turn of events. It was shortly after my grandfather's death and the resulting argument that my dad was diagnosed with cancer. I will say it here and now, cancer sucks.

It seems that it is so easy to get the diagnosis of cancer but getting started on treatment took forever. Dad was a little complicated with some thyroid issues that needed to be resolved before any treatment. Some tough decisions were made. After many months, he had surgery for the cancer and then started radiation. He was lighthearted throughout and encouraged. His results for the cancer were not as encouraging as he was hoping. The cancer spread to his spine. He went on to take chemotherapy. The chemo made him weak. He was nauseated and his brain was foggy. He was in pain, a shell of himself.

Dad announced to the family that he was discontinuing the chemo. He was done. He didn't like the way he felt. This upset the entire family, especially my older sister, Penny, who wanted him to keep fighting. She hated his decision. She hated him for not trying. However, after he stopped the chemo, he had quality of life. He was able to get out of bed, eat his meals at the table, and get outdoors into his garden. The garden was his place to go to think, harvest from the earth, and be peaceful.

When the time came, we were all by my dad's side when he passed. He looked around and took inventory of his family who came to say goodbye. Once everyone was present, he took his last breath. It was done. He was out of pain. That was twenty-one years ago.

My sister, Penny, passed away from lung cancer ten years after Dad passed away. She was only fifty-three years old. This was a déjà vu moment. Her cancer surfaced after a stressful time in her life. It was about events around her daughter and grandson. My sister was my best friend. I miss her horribly. We were five years apart, and after Courtney died, she helped bring me to God. Penny was an awesome sister. We loved to play softball, scrapbook, and talk on the phone for hours. Our favorite pastime was our annual baking. We would get together to bake cookies, dozens of them, multiple varieties. We kept our heritage going by baking Swedish Tea Rings, a wonderful bread with brown sugar, cinnamon, and walnuts. Our mom taught us how to do that and the ladies of the house got together to do this every year. My sister taught me love, compassion, and to stand up for myself. I miss her horribly and nobody, nobody can replace her.

Family death has become a part of my life. My mom passed away in 2016 from lung cancer – a third person in my family to die from cancer. May I repeat: cancer sucks. Mom was eighty-four years old. Hers was a long battle with poor health, lack of quality of life, and multiple illnesses. Mom was the one who wore her heart on her sleeve. She worried about all of us. She wanted the best. She helped us when we were down. Mom outlived Dad, something I thought would never happen. I love my mom. I see myself in her. I see her in me.

She was ready to move on. Her life was miserable. I often joked with her, "If you were a horse, we would have shot you years ago to take you out of your pain." She understood. We have more empathy for an animal that suffers than a human that suffers. I share this because it is me. It is how I think. I voice my opinion and am not afraid to be judged by others. It is important that I am able to be who I am.

I AM A SURVIVOR. I AM RESILIENT. I AM OPTIMISTIC.

In the span of twenty-seven years I have lost two children, both parents, and a sister, and gone through a divorce. That doesn't even count in-laws, nieces, and cousins. This story is about how I survived loss, how resiliency has helped, and how my optimism moves me forward.

When I share my story, I am often told I have "been through a lot." When I look at it from others' perspectives, I guess you could say I have been through a lot. The funny thing is it is my norm. My life includes the death of children, parents, and siblings. I am asked how I have made it through my life this far with all this bad stuff. When I look at how, I see that my upbringing, training, and attitude are my rocks, my foundation for survival. The cool thing is that I will share these things with you.

BLESSED WITH ANSWERS

Courtney was the first in this series of family deaths. The pain is less. I still think about her, maybe even more so since Connor passed. With each death, I acquired new tools to lean on to conquer the grief. One tool is my ability to focus on a purpose to live. Who am I living for? Who am I helping? I find when I take the focus off myself, my grief, my pain lessens. Sometimes we see that our circumstances are worse than others' and we can be grateful for what we have. My purpose has changed over time. My purpose is now to help others work through their grief and be happy again.

Just like my mom, I am vulnerable and openly share my feelings. I wear my heart on my sleeve. I let others see who I am. I cry in public. If someone asks why the tears, I share that I am crying because I miss my son. I started blogging my thoughts on Facebook. My readers see how my heart aches, but they also see how I deal with it. I am not afraid to tell someone "I love you." I express my fears, doubts, and dreams. It is not all the bad things. Sharing the good is equally important as well. Being vulnerable has helped in my loss journey.

Twelve-step recovery programs have been great tools in my toolbox. I first started attending Al-Anon in 1998. I realized that Jesse was an alcoholic and I needed to do something. Al-Anon is a partner program for friends and family of alcoholics. I started attending because I was at a loss as to what to do. Our marriage was in trouble. The biggest takeaway at the time was to trust in your higher power. It was a long time coming but the pieces came together for my God. Penny stuck with me and it was time to release everything to God. It was about the same time that Dad was starting his health challenges. Al-Anon brought me to my God.

I had another opportunity to tap into a twelve-step program when both Brittany and Connor entered Cornerstone, an alcohol and drug recovery program for youth. I participated in the parent companion twelve-step program and learned many valuable tools. One of those tools is to "take what you like and leave the rest." With this principle, you may not like everything you hear. You may like only one or two ideas. Only part of it may be something you can apply in your circumstances. That is what it means. Take the parts you like, apply them or keep them for later use and leave the rest.

Another principle is the "three Cs." You can't control things. You can't change things. You didn't cause this to happen.

What happens behind the scenes of entrepreneurship is more than I signed up for. I started my entrepreneurial career because I wanted to help others. I wanted to make a difference in their health and wellness. I didn't know I would have to learn new skills. I returned to college to gain the skills as a personal trainer. I learned about muscle groups, heart rates, metabolism, and nutrition. I learned how to write great workouts for weight loss and strength gains. I learned how to work with different populations: seniors, pregnant women, youth, and everyone in between.

What I didn't learn was how to build a business. Basic business building skills I needed included marketing and relationships. I had to believe in myself and believe in my company. I intentionally sought ways to learn those skills. I have been blessed with fantastic business and personal development resources. I have worked with multiple coaches, participated in numerous seminars and enjoyed learning about vulnerability.

To this day, I use many of the tools and techniques which I acquired through my lifetime I find the opportunity to learn something daily. This gives me the chance to add to my toolbox so that I am better equipped to help others. I never understood the power of these outside of my business until Connor passed. However, unknowingly, I have been tapping into them for years.

Most of my adult life, I have been highly aware of self-care, self-care that includes exercise, proper nutrition, sleep, water, and mental health. These have been my passion and go-to in times of trouble. I know that being proactive with my health is one of the many tools that help me. It is with great pleasure that I will be sharing how they have assisted in my grief process.

PUT YOUR OXYGEN MASK ON FIRST

I like to recount the pre-flight instructions that we get every time we board an airplane. "Ladies and gentlemen, in the event the oxygen masks drop, please place it on yourself first before helping anyone else." This is not a selfish move. You can't help others if you are unconscious. Put your oxygen mask on so you help yourself so you can help others. I am convinced there is someone out there who needs you. Do not cheat them by not taking care of yourself.

Today, even though it has been only fourteen months since Connor took his life, I find joy in every day. Honestly, some days are a struggle, but I work on it. The journey has changed me. I fondly remember my sister, parents, and children. I have several reasons to live. I have two beautiful daughters and a grandson on the way. I am now the matriarch of my family and I don't take it lightly. One of my favorite sayings is, "If Momma Bear ain't happy, then nobody is happy." Whatever led you to read this book, it is about taking care of yourself and seeking the opportunity to heal.

3

THE FRAMEWORK FOR REGAINING JOY AFTER CHILD LOSS

This pain has been forced upon you; you did not have a say in it. But the journey you're about to embark upon is your choice. A journey of healing is never an easy one. I do promise that if you are open to the journey, things can and will change and get better. What is on the other side of that long rocky road is hope, peace, and joy. It is a journey that never ends. It just gets less bumpy. The alternative is a sorry state of living. I don't say that to scare you. I say it because I am honest. I've seen it happen. I've seen parents, relationships, and marriages destroyed by the loss of a child. Do not let the death of your child dictate your happiness for the rest of your life.

I will say this time and time again – what I am offering is the framework that helped me move forward on my loss journey. This framework comes from experience. I believe that someone like myself who has life experience versus formal specialized college training and certifications can be the best person to walk beside you in a tough season. Congratulations on taking a big step. It is not easy to recognize or admit that you can use some help.

Each process in the framework does not work in isolation. They overlap and you will probably visit each step more than once. I found that depending on where I am in my grief, there was a step or tool that was much more relevant and useful in the moment. Tap into the steps as you deem necessary. There is no right or wrong order. I encourage you to read the entire book and come back to it for reference often.

If you have a print copy of this book, highlight what is important, write in the margins your thoughts, or dog-ear the pages. If you are reading it digitally, I suggest you have a notebook to take notes in. There is an abundance of useful information that will help you heal. When you need that tool, the last thing you want to do is search for answers. Keep them at your fingertips.

With each step, a new set of emotions may surface, or it may be some of the same old ones. Either way, going through these steps will support you in facing those emotions. Emotions come out wherever you are. It is good to learn to cope with them instead of sweeping them under the rug. You will find out more about yourself than you ever imagined. You have been changed by the loss of your child and you have the chance to grow, be better and make a difference. You will have the courage and strength to face your emotions and what lies ahead.

The framework is meant to ease the grieving process. It will not take away the pain. Intentionally work the steps. Put into action what you learn. When you are amidst a grief wave, you will have tools to tap into. You will have resources available at your fingertips. Learn them. Use them. They will support you.

There are eight steps in the framework for regaining joy after child loss. These came together as I have been going through my current loss journey. It is a melting pot of tools and resources that helped me. Some are tried and true while others are new. I can say they work together. You may find one piece more useful than another. I am okay with that. I am thrilled to share with you what worked for me.

THE FRAMEWORK

Journaling is the opportunity to put on paper your thoughts, create clarity, and express your emotions. This is the perfect place to start your journey as a loss traveler. Here is a safe place to begin processing what has happened.

Find your support system to connect with in the moments of desperation and in times of light. They will be with you now and forever. Your tribe is what will keep you going and keep you from feeling alone.

Develop a relationship with God or your higher power. Actively seek God and understand He is the healer and you can be healed through His mighty hand. You may have difficulty with the why of your loss. You can turn to God and lean into Him for understanding. Here you may find purpose in your life.

Learn how to talk about your child without guilt, bring joy, and teach others how to help you in this process. This so-called elephant in the room can be removed and you will be able to share memories and not be upset or embarrassed.

Learn how to deal with your child's possessions. Explore ideas on what is the right move for your child's belongings. This is an individual process. Stories and examples will help you decide what to do.

Understand how grief impacts holidays, birthdays, and anniversaries. Be prepared for what they bring and create a plan to get through them. You will learn how to anticipate these special days so rather than creating pain, you will be able to make it through them with joy.

Use self-care to help in your grief. Gain clarity on the

importance of taking care of yourself and give yourself the best fighting chance to physically survive this season. This is an area often overlooked. However, you will feel empowered to take charge of your health.

Be open to personal growth. Your life has been forever changed. Grab this opportunity to become a stronger, better you. It may be difficult now to think about what it looks like. You will gain insight into what your options are.

While writing this book, even before the framework was organized I realized how many people I already helped. The friend that I helped the most, Joanne, shared she had given up on life. She was no longer making herself a priority. She saw her health decline, her depression deepen, and was no longer happy. She didn't like the decisions she was making. She found she was not living the life she wanted.

She lost a nephew in a car accident several years before. He was her favorite nephew and they were close. They did so much together. She was helping him study for his college entrance exams. He wanted to attend the same college she did. He helped her with chores around her house and they both had a love for techno concerts. I understood why she was grieving and also told her that she could find the same happiness she had prior to his death.

We spent some time talking about choices and what the consequences are, both the positive and negative. Initially, she felt she was handling the loss of her nephew quite well. She became a workaholic, spent less time at home with her husband and children. When she was home, she was in her home office working late into the night, missed meals with her family, and was at the office before anyone was up. She shared with me that she was hiding behind her work. She did not want to face the reality of his death. She was angry with the man who caused the accident. She wasn't able to talk about it. She stuffed all her emotions and feelings. Taking a closer look at her behavior, she realized she was not dealing with the loss at all.

I told her about Courtney and Connor, what I was doing and how it was working for me. At that time, I could give her an overview of journaling, experience with my birthday, and how I was using the twelve steps. The chasm between Courtney and Connor was being bridged by my attitude and perseverance. I told her that I was not looking for perfection, rather for progress. I knew she could do the same. She had a choice to make.

She shared her desire to find her relationship with her husband and children. She decided to stop taking on extra work, leave work at the office, and set aside time to be with her family. She also started writing down her goals. She now had the time and purpose to move forward. She didn't feel like she was dishonoring her nephew but rather honoring him. To live a fulfilling life is something he would have wanted her to do.

Use the framework to guide you in discovering a purpose to move forward. Remember that you are not alone on this journey. I share my stories and journey to demonstrate you can not only survive this journey, but you can thrive. If I can do it, you can do it. Your story is different. It is unique. However, the framework applies to you too. There is hope, and I believe in you. You can regain joy after losing your child.

Take my hand, and let's do this together.

4

START WITH JOURNALING

It sucks that you are in this place. You did not expect to be here. No one ever expects to have a child die before them. It is just not the order. It is not something you plan for or ever get training on how to handle. It is one of those circumstances that you learn as you go. After Connor died, I was distraught and confused. I didn't know what direction to go and I went back to something I have done throughout the years, starting with Courtney. I turned to writing down my thoughts.

Journaling is the first step of the process for regaining joy after child loss. Why journaling? To be honest, it is the easiest of all things to do. It is accessible to everyone. All you need is a pencil or pen and paper. It can be taken anywhere and done anytime. There is no right or wrong.

HOW CAN JOURNALING HELP IN YOUR GRIEF?

Having gone through the loss of my first daughter, I know that my friends find it difficult to understand the grief and heartache of me, a grieving parent. They will never fully understand. I found it hard to talk to them, to convey how I felt. Writing down my thoughts in whatever way they spilled out of my head helped me to feel like somebody truly understood, even if that somebody was a pad of paper. The paper didn't judge. The journal is a safe place to express thoughts. It is the best friend because it holds my secrets, my fears, my anger, and my heartache.

There were many times that I cried as I wrote. Tears often stained the page and blurred the ink. It didn't matter how the page looked. My thoughts were out of my head. Writing down my thoughts often left me exhausted while at the same time helping me to heal.

WHAT KIND OF JOURNAL?

Buy a notebook that will be special to you. You may want a simple school composition notebook or one that is colorful, possibly with flowers or a design that makes you feel good. You can get the wide-ruled or college lines. I use the wide-ruled because when I am on a roll with my writing, my words get big and take up a lot of room. I need some structure with the lines, but you may find a blank notebook suits your needs. Choose whatever is right for you.

Grab several pens because you want to make sure that they work. When your thoughts are flowing freely, you don't want to run out of ink. You may find different colored inks also help. If you are feeling a particular emotion, you may want to use a certain color.

If you are concerned about keeping your journal safe, there are a couple of options to ensure that it is for your eyes only. You can purchase a file box that has a lock and key and keep it in there. You can also purchase a journal that has a lock on it. A journal has your deepest innermost thoughts so make sure it is in a place you feel secure.

HOW TO JOURNAL

When you sit down to write, find a place that is safe to express your emotions. They will come out on paper and come out physically. Journal at the same time daily. I prefer to write every morning before I get out of bed. Well, almost. I grab a cup of tea then crawl back into bed to write. My notebook and pens sit on my nightstand, so I know where they are. Journal when the time is right for you. If you want to jot down your thoughts while they are fresh, then carry your journal with you. Before bed may be the right time for you to let go of the day's events. Multiple entries may be what you need. Whenever or how many times you journal is up to you.

Journaling is a free flow of your thoughts. There is no judgment, right or wrong, punctuation, or time limit. Feel free to cuss. Open your heart and let the pen flow. The only thing I recommend is to start each entry by dating it. Add the time if writing several times during the day. This will be helpful later.

After that, it is all about how you feel. If you are angry, write it down. Include why you are angry. It seems like the obvious reason that you are angry is because your child is gone. Yes, that is the truth, but as we grieve, we can lash out to others in anger. Maybe someone cut you off in traffic, maybe someone was rude to you, maybe your husband doesn't understand why you didn't make dinner and stayed in your pajamas all day. You may be feeling guilty for what happened. The guilt as a parent, repeatedly asking why this happened is one of the worst feelings. Write it down. You may be sad. What triggered your sadness? Write it down. By getting it down on paper, you can process your thoughts and emotions and see you are not insane. Get it all out.

You may want to talk to your child. As weird as it seems, I often document conversations with Connor. Write a letter to your child. I get to say things I wish I had said when I had the chance. I tell him I miss him. I also share what happened during the day. Yes, it is a one-sided conversation, yet it allows me to feel connected. Write it down. I believe your child hears and sees you. Let them know you still love them and think of them.

Confusion and desperation can seep into your thoughts. You may not know what to do next. Write it down, including any possible solutions or ideas. Seeing things on paper helps with clarity. To see them written down helps to visualize the extent of them. You can use that later to put things in order or decide what your next step is.

Journaling is also a place to remember your loved one. I think one of the greatest fears of a parent is that their child will be forgotten, that the memories will fade away. With that fear, we try to keep all those memories in our heads at all times, which is impossible to do. Write down memories so that they are preserved forever. As you write, there will be more times, places, and events that pop into your head. Write these down too and remember the happy times, the times spent together. This will enable you to come back to revisit at any time you desire.

Three months after Connor passed away, I went on a three-week road trip. I called it the "road trip to recovery." This came together in less than a week. In spite of protests from friends and family concerned about my safety, a woman traveling alone, I took off. I felt deep down it was what I needed. This time would help me reflect, deepen my relationship with God, and heal. It was something I was led to do alone. A friend offered to go with me, and even though it would have been great to have her join me, I held true to my purpose.

I stayed with friends and family. I stayed in a raunchy Airbnb and a lavish bed and breakfast. I wanted to make it an experience of a lifetime. I did not have a specific agenda. I was spontaneous and enjoyed my flexibility. I stopped at historic sites, took random pictures, and went on many, many hikes. Being outdoors is where I ground myself. I appreciate the beauty and commune with God. God talks to me by revealing His majesty.

Without the chatter and activity of the daily grind, I was able to think about the future. What did my future look like without Connor? What did my future look like with my girls? How was I going to make it through this season? This all went into my journal.

I am surprised about the things that came out of my road trip. I saw small shifts in the way I was thinking. I was able to start to think about how Connor's death was impacting me, what my new purpose in life was. It was here that the idea of writing this book was born.

By now you see that anything goes when you are journaling. It is a free flow of your thoughts, expressing whatever comes to mind. It is a safe place. You can cry and most likely will. It is a way to heal. It is the simplest of all ways to start the process of your loss journey.

MEASURE YOUR PROGRESS

Remember when I suggested to date your journal entries? Go back to the beginning and look at them. Looking back at your entries is a measurement of your progress. It is an evaluation of where you are in the journey. The progress is yours to see. Nobody else is measuring it. It is for you only.

How often you look back depends on your desire to see your progress. In the first few weeks, you may not see or feel any. At the month mark, you may see an ever so slight shift in your thinking. I saw a transition at three months. I was coming to terms with my loss and able to look at my future.

There are two general directions of progress you may experience. The first is that things are getting better. I am not saying that you will ever get over the loss of a child. What I am saying is that you are starting to move through this season. You may notice that you are not as sad every day. The tears may be less. You are able to see some happiness in the day. You may see some hope of a future. You may see light. You may want to do more. By going back and reading my entries, I noticed small increments of progress. Initially, I described my pain and heartache. There were times I couldn't see through the tears to write, then I started including what I was grateful for instead of only focusing on the sadness. I found great relief when I started using metaphors. This is one of my favorite ones:

"Something about dead trees grabs my attention with their knots, twisted branches, and uprooted roots. There is an artistic beauty in them. God created them. In life they provided shade and shelter from storms and protected the landscape with their lives. It was when they lost their battle with Mother Nature that they now serve a different purpose. As a broken, fallen tree they supply shelter for the smallest animals. As they rot, they provide nutrients to fertilize the soil and provide new life and new beginnings."

As I pondered on this thought, it came to mind that Courtney's and Connor's lives were like the fallen trees. They had great lives, impacted and influenced others around them. This comforted me that in their short life spans, they made a difference. I found my days were better, even if only slightly. I could laugh. I could smile. The darkness was less. I saw all this through my writing.

The second path could be depression or clinically complicated grief. You may find yourself isolated, crying even more, and thinking things will never get better. You may even think about ending your life and that you want to be with your child. You may feel depressed. Grief has many layers and depression is not a normal part of it. Rather it is an impediment to moving through grief.

It is important to understand the difference between normal grief from depression by looking for specific emotional patterns.

It is important to understand what type of grief you are experiencing. Generally, grief is categorized as either normal or complicated.

According to Sydney Zisook, MD, "In normal grief, the sad thoughts and feelings typically occur in waves or bursts followed by periods of respite, as opposed to the more persistent low mood and agony of major depressive disorder."

Complicated grief is a form of persistent, pervasive grief that does not get better naturally. It happens when "some of the natural thoughts, feelings, or behaviors that occur during acute grief gain a foothold and interfere with the ability to accept the reality of the loss," says Katherine Shear, MD, professor of psychiatry at Columbia University's School of Social Work and director of its Center for Complicated Grief.

Stephanie Hairston wrote in a WebMD article on grief in the body: "Symptoms of complicated grief include persistent efforts to ignore the grief and deny or 'rewrite' what happened. Complicated grief increases the risk of physical and mental health problems like depression, anxiety, sleep issues, suicidal thoughts and behaviors, and physical illness."

If you are experiencing these thoughts, please seek professional help, a counselor, psychiatrist, or psychologist. I do know that most mental health professionals encourage journaling so keep up with this step as you seek out additional help. They may want to review your journal with you to look for thought patterns. When you are too close to the circumstances, you may not see a repeating thought. You may not see you are a danger to yourself. This can guide how they work with you. You may have also expressed the intensity of your pain, which leaves hints of where you most need to focus.

FACEBOOK

Another option to privately journaling is going public to social media. This is quite the opposite of the privacy of the nightstand journal. Everyone in the world can see your thoughts. Facebook is an amazing place to share news. It is here that I posted about Connor and spread the news about his memorial service.

I posted my journey on Facebook. My initial posts were all about the pain, the tears, and the grief. I don't even know why. I guess because I felt like I had a community of people to share with what was going on in my life. I was vulnerable and shared my innermost thoughts. I had people respond to me with words of encouragement. Others responded they were experiencing the same thing. I started to get relief by sharing. Even if it is just a shout into the void, it can help release whatever is bubbling inside of you. Below are some of my posts.

December 19, 2018 (Five days after Connor died.)

"I can't make sense of the loss of my son, Connor Green, or see what the good is supposed to be."

April 28, 2019

"It is not the critic who counts. It is not the man who points out how the strong man stumbles or where the doer of deeds could have done it differently. The credit belongs to the person in the arena, whose face is a marred with dust, sweat and blood, who strives valiantly, who errors, who comes up short time again, again and again and in the end while he may know the triumph of high advancement at least when he fails, he does so daring greatly," Theodore Roosevelt, 1910.

Those who try and fail – it takes courage to do so. Courage means you will fall, you will stumble, you will fail because there is no guaranteed or certain outcome, there is risk and being emotionally battered is pretty certain. Courage is to rise above the critics, rise above the uncertainty and rise above the potential emotional pain.

Why do I bring this up? Friends keep telling me I am an inspiration and they admire my courage to be vulnerable and expose my pain. I appreciate everyone's support. Believe me though, I dig deep to be courageous. I know that what I say does not always sit well with others when I speak of my grief journey. They question, "How can she be doing so well? It has only been four months since her son passed away. How can she be happy and have joy in her life? She should still be grieving."

Joy can be scary to feel amidst grief. It can be scary to think my joy will never return. It can be scary to think my joy will be stolen again. Yet I make a choice and rise to have joy. How do I regain my joy? I lean into gratitude. I am grateful for the day. I am grateful for the sun. I am grateful for my family. I am grateful that I know a kind and loving God. My list can go on forever on the tough days, it is just to be grateful that I simply have a bed to sleep in, water to drink, and clothes to wear. You see, it is impossible to have two opposing emotions at the same time. I replace sadness with gratitude which gives way to joy. May you find joy in your life by starting with gratitude.

Journaling on my road trip helped me realize I got what I wanted, didn't get what I was looking for, and received more than I expected. Let me explain. I expected to be healed on my road trip. I wasn't. I got the time alone to process which is what I wanted. I was looking to be happy and normal when

I returned home. I wasn't. I discovered my loss journey would be a lifelong lesson in courage, strength, compassion, and understanding. I wasn't looking for courage or to be strong but those are the things that were given to me.

A MESSAGE OF HOPE

One of the most impactful messages was from a woman I had known for at least six years. I had no idea she was struggling. I received this message on Thanksgiving, less than one year after Connor passed.

> "Greetings and Happy Thanksgiving. I'm writing because I am pretty sure your son wanted me to. This morning as I was texting a message to my cousin, I started typing the word 'coming' I think and Connor came up in the predictive words. I don't have anyone in my life named Connor and until now I don't think I've ever typed it. So his name showing up is out of the ordinary. I'm taking this opportunity to thank you for sharing your grief the way you do. I've been hospitalized multiple times after suicide attempts and seeing your raw pain helps remind me how I'd be hurting my loved ones if I ever succumbed. I am in awe of your strength and grace and truly hope sharing your grief is healing to you. Have a wonderful Thanksgiving."
>
> — LYNN, FACEBOOK FRIEND

Whether you choose to write in a journal and keep it private, share on social media, or a combination of both, writing down and expressing your thoughts is a great way to get started in your healing journey. When you start to heal, there is a glimmer of hope, a ray of sunshine and purpose no matter how small or big, keep writing. You may not see it now, but you will be able to look back and see your story that helped you to heal.

JILL'S STORY

I have friends across the world. As they watch my journey and read my Facebook posts, many have reached out to me for support and guidance. My friend Jill, who lives in Illinois, has struggled with mental health. I suggested she journal. It is a work in progress. She has started and stopped several times. Currently she is journaling again. When we chatted, she discovered that when she is putting her thoughts on paper, they do not seem as scary as she made them out to be. She has been able to sort out the truth and the lies she has been telling herself. She likes to journal at night because she reflects on the day's activities. Instead of trying to hold onto everything, she releases them into her journal. If she thinks she has been "bad" during the day, she asks God for forgiveness. As a result, she goes to sleep with a clear conscious and rests well.

5

FIND YOUR TRIBE

INNER CIRCLE

I mentioned in Chapter 4 that others will have a difficult time relating to what you are going through. Because they don't understand, many of my friends and family withdraw. They are afraid they are going to cause more harm than good. They are afraid to say or do the wrong thing. They don't know how to help, so instead of asking how to help, they simply disappear. They return to their lives while you struggle to make sense of your loss.

One of the things that helped me the most was finding my tribe, my community of those people that I could count on. Relying on past experience, I knew what to expect from others. I knew I would need to find new people who I could relate to, who would speak the same language and who would understand the level of pain and grief I was going through. Some of my friends who I was the closest to are no longer around.

The loss of a child scares other parents. They can't imagine losing their child. I think they try to feel my pain which causes them to run. I call these folks “runners.” At the mention of the death of my child, I find myself consoling them. Now that is backward if I say so myself. I’ve seen tears in their eyes, conversations suddenly end, and an urgency to leave arises. They do anything to get away from a grieving mother. If I can’t count on my friends, who can I count on?

Don’t be totally discouraged, you will have a few friends that stick with you no matter what. These are the inner circle of friends. Hold them close and tell them what you need. I have one friend that I call my “crying friend.” Quite often, my grief would hit me late in the afternoon while I was driving. None of my friends were geographically close so the best I could do was talk on the phone. I have one friend that I could call anytime. I knew that when she answered the phone, I could tell her, “All I need you to do is listen to me cry.” I expressed my need and she did exactly as I asked. We couldn’t be together, but she could help by listening. Once I got through my cry, she asked me questions. “What triggered your grief today? How can I help?” I would share the situation and I felt close to her. I felt like she cared. After a few more minutes, she would have me laughing over some stupid stuff. She was one of those that stuck around.

Another friend who has been with me through both losses brings up my children. She helps by talking about Courtney and Connor. Sometimes she remembers stuff that I long ago forgot. She also checks in with me to see how I am doing. What am I thinking? How can she help me? I am eternally grateful to her.

A mother’s pain is different than that of a sibling. I don’t expect my two daughters to be my support alone. I know they need to find their way. I must admit that I am a bit jealous of another lifelong friend who has strong support from her family in the grief process. Her family is close, and they talk about their loved ones. We don't talk about them as much as I would like. I wish we could heal more as a family.

It is difficult to describe what I want. I just want to be with my girls more often and spend more time together. I am taking baby steps on organizing dinner and activities with them. Maybe it is not that I am grieving but rather I am working to keep what is left of my family together. Your family, brothers, sisters, parents, or spouse could be part of your tribe. Just because it is not the strongest part of my community, doesn't mean it isn't right for you. Look for those connections and support. However, if they don't understand your needs, look for your community in other places.

GRIEF GROUPS

Losing a child is devastating. There are communities designated just to address the topic of child loss. I am a part of multiple Facebook groups of this kind. I partake in them with caution because it is easy to get caught up in the grief trap. The grief trap is a place where loss travelers get stuck in their heartbreak. They don't have a sliver of hope or light that life can and will get better. I feel for them. Losing a child sucks. I understand their pain. I hope that someday they will find the courage to take a step toward healing. Be cautious and find a group that supports you and where you want to go. My main goal in these groups is to offer encouragement and be the lantern to a better place.

I sought out a local grief group. They met once a week and followed a faith-based curriculum. I loved the God-centered teaching, but the timing wasn't right. I found a group setting like this was not for me. It was an established group that knew each other and was in sync with knowing how to support each other. I felt like an outsider, but it is information I kept. There may be a day when that is the type of support I need.

The point is not to give up and to give grief groups a chance. Community is an essential part of your healing as I will explain in more detail below.

THE COMMUNITY MELTING POT

Some of my best supporters have come from Facebook. As I've posted about my journey, others with similar experiences reached out to me to share their stories. We connected over the club we now belong to. I support them and they support me. We see each other on Facebook, send private messages, and pray for each other.

I also found community in my church. Connor's memorial service was held at the church I attend. The women who gathered to help with the service and reception are amazing. I also had people "circle up" around me at church. My church family still prays for me. They never stop. I continue to receive messages that my family is being prayed for. This form of community is one of support through prayer. I don't know many of them but know them through God and their virtual support.

My franchise and business partners support me in a different way. After Connor passed away, I received a phone call from the corporate office expressing their condolences. I must say that was a moment that I am proud of because the company cared enough to call me. My business partners support me when I struggle with day-to-day duties. They help to keep me accountable. I've told them I want to continue to work and help others. One of my mentors says, "Help others and take the focus off your own problems." His thought-provoking comment has helped me to look beyond my problems and be able to help others.

I could go on for days about the tribe that surrounds me, so let's talk about the importance of having a community of supporters.

WHY IT IS IMPORTANT TO SURROUND YOURSELF WITH YOUR TRIBE

Having others around you can help prevent isolation. They must reach out to you and you have a network to reach out to. Having gone through this twice now, I can confidently say it is easy to push everyone away, especially those you are close to. However, those important people need help in helping you. Be vulnerable and express your needs. It is okay to ask for help with meals, laundry, and groceries. You may find it difficult to go out in public, so have someone go with you. Someone who will be there if you start to cry, someone who will tell you that you will be okay.

When we connect with others who have lost a child, it raises our awareness of the pain and suffering. This can help us to be much more empathetic to others in their journey. You can easily put yourself in their shoes. You can reach out to offer them words of encouragement, hope, and healing.

I've mentioned numerous places I found support from my tribe. Look for your inner circle, those who stick with you no matter what. Those you thought were your closest friends may not be able to deal with your grief. Family may not be able to give you the support you need. Understand they don't know how so don't expect them to. It is far better to adjust your expectations than to change the people. If you have established friendships through social media, you may find that is a good option. I do recommend not blowing up your page with all negative thoughts. Your friends like to encourage you and see your progress. Co-workers may be a good opportunity for new tribe. You never know who else may have experienced child loss. Once it is out in the open, people are so willing to share their stories and support each other.

I truly enjoyed working as a personal trainer. It was exactly that: personal. My clients and I established relationships beyond fitness. We became friends. My clients frequently shared intimate details of their life. It is not by accident that two separate clients revealed that a family member was struggling with alcohol abuse. These women were beside themselves and not sure what to do. Since I had been in the same position years earlier, I was able to let them know about Al-Anon. Both of them started attending meetings and learned the principles of being related to an alcoholic. The members of those meetings became part of their tribe while I supported them outside the meetings. We discussed the twelve steps, and I helped them "let go and let God." This is a slogan which helps to be responsible for what is rightfully yours and let God take over for the rest. Once a member of a twelve-step program, always a member with friendships and resources. The passing of your child creates an elephant in the room, making everyone uncomfortable and unwilling to talk about your child. That is exactly why I am dedicating the next step in our framework to talking about it.

6

TALKING ABOUT THE ELEPHANT IN THE ROOM

I never understood what "the elephant in the room" meant until Courtney died. It is that "thing" that everyone knows, but won't talk about.

Courtney became the "elephant in the room." She wasn't talked about. I felt as if in other people's minds she never existed. She did exist though. It was a short nine months, but she was here. I know because I birthed her. She laughed, she ate, she made me smile. She made her mark on my life. She left a piece of her with me. I don't understand why people don't want to talk about her. It confuses me and breaks my heart. However, this type of behavior is the status quo around the loss of a child. As a parent, talking about a child helps the grieving process. It helps to know your child will be remembered.

Jesse's family was especially good at not talking about Courtney. Grandma Green had a decorative apple tree with all the names of her grandchildren. When Brittany and Connor were old enough to read, Courtney's little apple was removed. Grandma didn't want questions to be raised as to who Courtney was. What bothered me was that all the cousins knew about her. They didn't talk about her either. But you ask why didn't Brittany and Connor know? It is because their dad refused to tell them or talk about her.

I was the one who finally took the initiative to tell them. Jesse wanted no part of it. By this time Hannah was two, Connor five, and Brittany six and a half years old. My sister made a photo album about Courtney and I used it to tell the kids. I sat down and shared that they had a sister, but she was in Heaven. I didn't know what to expect with the older two. I knew Hannah would grow up with Courtney's name being spoken. Courtney wouldn't be the elephant in the room for her. Connor somewhat understood and like Hannah, learned to speak Courtney's name.

Brittany, on the other hand, was quite devastated. She was sad to know she had a big sister she would never meet. She wondered what she looked like; would they be best friends? Questions that I often ask. This was a traumatic experience for Brittany to learn but it opened the doors to be able to openly talk about Courtney, making it no longer necessary to remove her apple when we visited Grandma.

Suicide is taboo to talk about. According to many people, suicide is a sin. Suicide is painful but it is not a sin. There is a hidden veil of shame to talk about someone who took their life. You just don't talk about it. After what happened with Courtney, I refused to not talk about Connor, regardless of how he died. I prefer to focus on how he lived.

Remember in Chapter 5 we discussed your tribe? They are a great place to talk about your child. You already established they are safe and genuinely want to help you. The people I tap into the most are my inner circle of friends. They know and understand me. They are loving and kind. They all knew Connor and most knew Courtney.

SUSIE'S STORY

Loss travelers are drawn to me. They don't know my circumstances, yet they are compelled to share theirs. A new friend recently told me about her husband's death. It had been well over ten years. While we were hiking, she shared her husband had passed. I felt a great sense of relief wash over her as she told me what happened. My heart went out to her. She is grateful that she and her children are able to talk about her husband and their father amongst themselves. However, it has been difficult to talk with other family members, not about his death but about his life. She so desperately wanted to recall the memories.

She told me she tried to talk about him at a family gathering. When she did, she received blank stares and silence. The conversation was quickly changed. I suggested that rather than speaking in a large group, that she talk about her husband one-on-one. That way, each person could share their memories and not feel judged by other family members.

Susie started with her brother-in-law, who she was still close to. That conversation went better than she could have hoped for. He wanted to talk about his brother also but felt he couldn't. Her conversation opened the door to move the family forward in talking about her husband, Joe. By not taking on the entire family at once, and starting with one person she can now openly talk about Joe with other family members. This makes her heart sing and she is so grateful she can share her memories.

WHY IT IS IMPORTANT TO CLEAR THE ELEPHANT IN THE ROOM

Knowing that you can freely speak your child's name is healing. It helps to know your child is being remembered. I share with friends that I do want them to talk about Connor. They share their memories about my children that I never knew about. It is the opportunity to see a piece of your child through someone else's eyes.

Sure, it may bring tears and tear open the wound, but each time the tears are smaller. Tears are healing. They have different chemicals depending on whether they are happy or sad tears. It is okay to cry. As a matter of fact, I encourage you to cry.

Talking about your child with a trusted friend gives you a safe place to acknowledge your feelings about your child. Just as when you are journaling, speaking it aloud can facilitate the emotions you are experiencing. Your tribe doesn't judge. Unlike the journal, they can give you feedback. They can be a sounding board. It creates a deeper bond between friends. It helps them too. They are grieving the loss of your child as well. My friends share that our conversations help them to help others. They now have my experiences to share and tap into.

CONVERSATIONS WITH A CHAPLAIN

You may also seek the help of a professional to speak about your child. I spent a lot of time talking to a chaplain (no, not the one at the emergency room). He helped me to find words to teach friends how to talk about my children. If your child passed by suicide, there are softer, gentler ways to say it. Rather than "committed suicide," say "died by suicide." An act of "committing" something" is a crime or a sin with a stigma attached. Other options are "took their life" or "killed himself."

The chaplain also changed the way I thought about Connor's death. Instead of saying "What if I had called him more" we changed it to "As if I had called him more?"

Instead of "What if I had known" we changed it to "As if I would have known?" "What if I had given him money" changed to "As if I had given him money." We took the "what if" out and changed it to "as if." As if I had known things would have turned out the same. It made all the difference in the way I thought. I was blessed with a connection to a chaplain.

He helped me understand some of the problems Connor was facing. He told me, "The troubles that were haunting Connor are no longer bothering him. Satan is no longer standing on his shoulder. He is at peace." That was a huge breakthrough for me.

ANSWERING "HOW MANY CHILDREN DO YOU HAVE?"

One of the hardest questions to answer is "How many children do you have?" In theory this is a simple question, but for a parent who has lost a child, it is not so easy to answer. The other person unknowingly opens Pandora's box. How I answer the questions depends on my relationship with the other person. Have they earned the right to see me at my worst moment? Will they judge me or turn away as I tear up? Other factors include the social setting in which the question is asked, where I am when asked the question, and my nanosecond judgment to determine if this is the right place and time to share. It also depends on if I feel mentally and emotionally prepared to accept their response. It isn't easy to decide how to answer a simple question. It is something you will deal with for the rest of your life. You may find having numerous responses is helpful.

One answer is to give the full response. If the stars are aligned and I am feeling comfortable, happy, and able to deal with their reaction, I say, "Two in Heaven and two on earth."

I wait and watch their face for their reaction, especially their eyes for tears. Many respond with "I can't imagine. That must be horrible." My typical response is "Yes, it is. It sucks." Sometimes they are curious and want to learn more. They ask questions about what happened. I don't offer details. Tell them the minimum. Courtney died in a daycare accident and Connor took his life. No matter how I share, they are shocked. I use my intuition to share more or stop. If you recall, I mentioned earlier in Chapter 5 that talking about your experience can create "runners." Telling someone that I have lost two children often creates a runner faster than a blink of an eye.

Another option to answering the question is to say four and leave it at that. I take the chance of them asking more questions. Sometimes they go on and ask about ages. If that happens, I share about the two in Heaven and two living. Then I am back to looking for their reaction to prepare for their next question.

If I feel we will never establish more than a passer-by relationship, I tell them two children. It makes it easy to talk about the living, their ages, where they live and what they do. Yes, at that point I took the easy way out.

Does this all seem in direct conflict with wanting to talk about my children? It may feel that way. As a loss traveler, there is no right or wrong way to grieve. It is your choice how and when to talk about your children, how many are alive, and how many in Heaven.

My higher power is God and that is why I talk about having children in Heaven. It is important for me to share because I am reassured that I will see them again. If you believe the same, it is possible for you to receive the same relief. Your higher power may not be God, but believing that you are not in control and there are other forces beyond you can offer guidance and relief to your grief.

7

HOW A HIGHER POWER CAN HELP YOU WITH YOUR GRIEF

TO BELIEVE OR NOT TO BELIEVE

A higher power is a supreme deity or other conceptions of God. Maybe you don't believe in God but that there is something bigger than you. It is what you turn to that explains the unexplainable. Your higher power is what gives you peace and rest. I believe in God and will refer to Him as such throughout the book. If that is not your belief, feel free to insert "higher power" when I describe God.

I've seen it happen time and time again. The death of a child changes a person. It changes their inner being, who they are, and what they believe. Those who once believed in God now scream out in anger asking "why." They ask how could a loving God allow this to happen. The pain is so great and the understanding so difficult that all faith in God is lost. Devout Christians with an unshakeable relationship with God suddenly dismiss their faith at the mention of His name.

On the opposite side of the coin are those who did not have any sort of faith in God but are drawn to Him in difficult times. A grieving parent may not have anywhere else to turn. God is their last resort in the suffering. They may have come to terms that they cannot survive this season without a supreme being that gives them strength and courage.

I was one of those kids who occasionally went to church with my mom. I attended a Lutheran church and went through confirmation, but it never carried into my adulthood. However, I did get married in a church. I think that was more because it was the thing to do. I didn't have a connection with God. After Courtney died, both my mom and sister invited me to church and to find God on a personal level. At the time, I wasn't ready to take the steps to move forward.

I started attending Al-Anon, which is a twelve-step program for friends and family of alcoholics. It was a huge resource for me as I was living with my alcoholic then-husband. About the same time my dad was diagnosed with cancer. One of the principles of Al-Anon is to find your higher power. That is what finally got me back to church. I used God as an excuse to get my kids to church. I told their dad it was to help when their grandfather passed. It was a cover for me to teach them about God and it was a place for me to seek support while living with an alcoholic. I went back to church for all the wrong reasons.

When Connor got big enough that I couldn't physically carry him to the car, he decided to stop attending church. His dad didn't support me taking the kids to church, so it was a tough battle that I lost. Connor did come to seek a higher power through the twelve-step programs he attended. He sometimes called the outdoors his higher power. It guided and directed him. I prayed that he would come to God someday. I was unsure if he believed in God or not.

What I do know is that on his playlist are some Christian songs. Songs about God and believing in more than the outdoors as his higher power. When I heard those songs, I knew that without a doubt he believed in God. Although he didn't publicly profess his belief, he believed. I can't say how happy I am to know that.

In April of 2018, I was baptized in a full immersion ceremony at my church. I had been attending church and developing a relationship with God, with Jesus. I wanted to publicly proclaim my belief in God. It was important that I set an example for my children. My family, including Connor, celebrated my baptism with me.

Wherever you are in your relationship with God, give Him some time to speak to you. God heals all wounds. He gives you the strength to pick yourself up. I relate to God and can't imagine being on this journey without Him. Surrender to God. Let Him help you. Let Him guide you. Let Him love you in a time when you can't love yourself.

Currently, I am following a program to read the entire Bible in a year. Each day is laid out with what chapter and verse to study. I am blessed to be doing this because this is the same list that my mom followed. I found it in her Bible after she passed away. It is not a coincidence it fell into my hands. My mother sent me a sign from Heaven that she is with me, always.

What happened is that I changed from being a "holiday" attender and believer to daily meditator, prayer warrior, and look for God to show Himself. It is absolutely amazing what happens when God is on my radar and how He reveals what I am supposed to see. He shows me only what is relevant. God has given me comfort in knowing He is the Almighty Healer. It is through Him that I have hope, peace and joy. I invite you to explore the possibilities.

MESSAGES FROM GOD

Over 300 people attended Connor's memorial service. The majority of those who attended were from school and numerous twelve-step programs he was involved with. The pastor who conducted the service shared with me his intuition that many of those who came were non-believers. He felt a sense of hatred toward God.

During his service he wanted to give them a way to understand that God was not responsible for Connor's death. He wanted to let them know that God was with him in his final moments, that God wouldn't just allow Connor to end his life. God was standing next to him, screaming in his ear "Don't do it. Don't do it. Don't do it." God could have stopped him, but He didn't. He let him follow his free will. That is one of the biggest things that has helped me to move through my grief. God did not kill my son. Connor killed himself. God is with me in my grief.

Another powerful message, I've previously mentioned, came from the chaplain. We would talk about Connor taking his life. What was going through his head and what he was experiencing had to be so bad that ending it all was the only way out. The pain must have been unbearable. The chaplain shared with me that whatever demons were haunting him were gone. They were no longer sitting on his shoulders and weighing him down. Satan no longer has a hold on him. God now has Connor in His arms. When I am having a tough time, I often revisit that conversation and thank God that Connor is at peace. Not only is he at peace but he is surrounded by his sister Courtney, Aunt Penny, Grandma, and Grandpa.

PRAYER

"Prayer is a solemn request for help or expression of thanks addressed to God or an object of worship. It is an earnest wish or hope," Merriam-Webster Dictionary

I find that praying is an opportunity to talk with God, tell Him what is on my mind and ask for help. Prayer is easy to do and can be as simple as saying the word "help." The Holy Spirit knows what is on your heart so even thinking a prayer counts. The Holy Spirit intercedes on your behalf and helps God to see your heart. Prayers do not have to be perfect. We can pray to God because Jesus took away that barrier and we have full access to the Father. Unlike our earthly fathers, God does not get mad when we are angry with Him. Instead He draws us closer.

Prayers can be said anywhere and anytime. There is no judgment. In fact, God *wants* us to talk to Him all the time. You can look for answers and find them. You can show your gratitude, talk about your fears, and ask for help.

TYPES OF PRAYERS

- Pour out your grief when your heart is filled with sadness and despair. You may be at a loss for words. In this type of prayer, you express to God what you are going through, talk to Him as you would a friend.

    - "Dear Lord, I am at a loss for words. I just know my heart is broken in a million pieces. You, the Almighty know what I am going through. Please help me understand."

• Ask for comfort as a way to reach out to God in your grief. Comfort is seeking freedom from your pain.

  ○ "Dear Heavenly Father, relieve me of the feelings of guilt and grief over the loss of my child."

• Ask for healing so that God brings His almighty powers to you. It is said, "knock and you shall receive." Knock with prayer and God will heal.

  ○ "God, I ask you to heal my broken heart that I will have the courage and the strength to carry on."

• Ask for peace against the confusion in your heart.

  ○ "Dear Lord, you are the Almighty. I need the inner peace that you alone can bring. Calm my anxious spirit. The 'if-onlys' and 'what-ifs' fill my heart with needless worry. Please take them away."

• Prayer for hope is the desire to have things change, get better.

  ○ "God, this is me, your servant and disciple. I am in a horrible place and I now plead you to give me hope for a better future, that I may see daylight again and I may find joy."

• God uses the brokenhearted as His way of making us strong. We may not see what the purpose is but God will reveal it.

  ○ "Dear Heavenly Father, I am broken, down on my knees and desperate. I don't understand why this is happening. I know that You use the brokenhearted to help others. I am having a tough time. Please reveal to me how You will use me and my grief for the good."

God is using me to help others in their loss journey. Without a doubt, I know that God has given me all the tools, resources, and beliefs to survive this season. God does not choose the strong to lead but gives the weak, broken, and tired the strength to lead. I am one of those weak, broken, and tired ones.

Before I sat down to write a chapter for this book, I prayed that God would give me the words, and through Him that others will heal. One of the strongest messages I received from Connor was that he was sorry. Had he known how much pain he is causing, his choice would be different. He didn't end his life to hurt us. He just couldn't handle his life circumstances any longer. Because of that, it is through me that he is not done on this earth. He is making a difference by helping others through their loss.

Be open to God as your higher power. If He isn't it, then seek a higher power. Surrendering control is not easy to do. It is one of the best things I've ever done. I must do it every day. It is easy to rise and start my day with my agenda. What are my plans? What are my goals? What am I going to accomplish? Then I realize it is not about what I want to do. It is about God's will. I must stop and ask God what His wish for me is. What does He want me to do? Surrendering is a process. Give control back to God. I am not in control. Ask God to help and openly give it to Him. Life goes so much better when I surrender.

It is important that I set the stage for my day. No matter what I do, I must be a servant of God. I am His messenger, His disciple, the example of a loving Christian woman. This book is my ministry and opportunity to do good on God's behalf. I ask God to tell me who He wants me to touch and impact for His glory.

If you are questioning if there is a God, visit several churches and find one you are comfortable with. Many churches offer classes to those who are checking out the possibility that God exists. Take the class and make the decision yourself. You may want to ask a friend to join you for moral support. Talking to God and expressing your deepest thoughts can be emotional.

In your darkest hour, you may feel buried and unable to cope. Think of yourself as a seed that has been planted in the soil. Seeds need to be in the dark for a season to sprout and grow. Look for what God is preparing you for. What plans does He have for you?

MEDIUMS

Building my belief in God has been easy compared to what I've learned about spirits, mediumship, and signs from the other side. A dear friend gifted me a reading with a medium to talk to Connor. At first, I was extremely hesitant because I thought it was satanic. I was led to believe that it was wrong. After much thought and prayer, I accepted the gift. The reading was to be done over the phone, so Brittany and Hannah were included in the session. We waited several months before having our reading. Connor wasn't ready to connect with us and I was skeptical. The medium we worked with is a strong Christian. It didn't feel wrong. It felt right.

As in any industry, there are reputable and non-reputable mediums. There are certifications and reputable groups. When contacting them, please confirm their credentials.

Our gifted medium explained that Connor probably would not use words; he would use pictures, signs, and places to respond to her connection. It wasn't like those scenes in the movies with someone with a crystal ball. The girls and I sat on the couch with the phone on the table with the speaker on so we all could hear what she said.

She started by being silent and allowing Connor to connect with her. The first thing he showed her was a brown bag. The brown bag was the darkness that he could not escape. He could not get away from it. He could not remove it. Therefore, his solution was to end it all. I can tell you, I had no idea he was in so much pain. He had shared some of it with Brittany in the week before his death but was nothing she felt would lead him to take his life. He also shared that he was sorry. He was sorry for the pain he was causing us. If he had known the pain it would put us through, he wouldn't have done it. We don't know what we don't know. I couldn't blame him for our pain. He didn't intentionally want to cause us heartache. He was in the moment and made a decision to end it all. He wasn't thinking clearly. There wasn't hope of getting out of the darkness. He just had to put an end to his suffering. While I don't agree with his decision I am grateful he is at peace. That I can accept.

SIGNS

I missed the first sign Connor ever sent to me because I wasn't looking for it. On the day of his funeral, I went for an early morning run. Running has always been an outlet and place to ground myself. That morning the sunrise was spectacular. It was one of the most beautiful ones I have ever seen. For a December day, it was unusually warm. The wind was still and the sky was filled with cotton ball clouds. As the sun peeked over the horizon, deep shades of orange, yellow, and black reflected off the clouds intensifying their hue. I had to stop my run and stand in awe of the beauty. I took a picture to add to my collection of them. If you were to ask me one of my favorite things, I would answer sunrise and sunset. You see, Connor and I shared the love of them. On that day, he was sending me a message that I would be okay, that he loved me, and that sunrises are his way to let me know he is with me. I didn't understand his message then but I do now.

What amazes me even more is Connor visits me without the help of a medium. Even before our session, he came to me by manipulating the energy (electrical power) with the lights in my China Buffet. Without anyone touching the light switch, it came on. The first time, I was startled and passed it off as a random occurrence. Since then, the light has come on by itself. I learned that those who are on the other side can and do send us messages. The purpose of the signs is to let you know they are with you, watching over you, and want to help you through your grief.

This concept has taken a while for me to grasp. I believe it happens though. A friend gave me a book about the signs from the other side. I devoured it in a few days and now look for them everywhere I go. I want to feel that connection. The things that I see are not random occurrences. Just the other day, I asked Connor to show me a lion. I saw a lion decal on the back of a car. Connor did not stop there though. He proceeded to put Simba from *The Lion King* into my head along with one of his favorite songs, "Hakuna Matata."

I am like a child when I learn something new. I want to share it with everyone. That is what I have done since learning about mediums and signs. In one of my Facebook support groups, several people mentioned they felt like their loved one was trying to give them a message. However, they were having a difficult time believing this could happen. We started chatting privately where I encouraged them to open their heart for signs. Jeannie replied, and since talking about signs, she replied, "My child was twenty-eight hours old when he passed away. I see shooting stars and I know it's him." Another woman, Taylor, shared she started seeing dragonflies. She saw them on the flowers outside of her front door, on the patio chair, and on her car windshield. Dragonflies were something her son loved and she was so happy to learn the signs from him.

You may be little skeptical about receiving signs and I understand. I suggest reading the book *Signs* by Laura Lynne Jackson and start looking for them. They have helped me tremendously.

Find your higher power. It may or may not be my God. Lean into it and ask for help. Be on the lookout for signs from the other side. If you have been journaling, you can keep track of them in there. If you aren't journaling, now would be a good time to start.

8

HOW TO DEAL WITH LOVED ONE'S BELONGINGS AND CREATING A MEMORIAL

FINGERPRINTS ON THE MIRROR

As a parent, once your child is gone, what you have left are memories and their possessions. You struggle to never forget even the simplest of memories and wrestle even more what to do with their things.

I remember Courtney's handprints on a floor-length mirror that hung on the wall at the foot of my bed. She was just starting to stand and needed to hang onto a wall to hold herself up. She loved it when she could see herself in the mirror. She would smile, giggle, and pat the baby in the mirror. Her handprints were placed there just days before she passed. They were a living memory of her. The picture of her so cute and happy in my head when I looked at those handprints meant I wanted to preserve them forever. It was also painful to see them every day and know she was gone. The conflict of grief and joy was ever so strong.

I decided to not wash them off and to leave them to remind me of her. I grew to appreciate their presence until one day I decided to clean the mirror. I planned to go around her tiny smudged fingerprints but instead with one fell swoop they were gone. Gone forever, just like her. I was devastated. I called my friend in a panic. How could I do this? What was I thinking? I was mad and angry at myself.

In spite of this gut-wrenching experience, I was able to forgive myself and remember her in other ways. I have a beautiful picture of her that captures her essence. It is even more special because it is in a dress that my sister bought for her. Now when I look at that picture, I see both Courtney and Penny and some memory will flash through my head and bring peace.

PASSING DOWN CLOTHES

Because Courtney was our first child, and I wanted more children, we saved the baby items. I kept the circus-themed decorations and blanket. When we got home from the hospital, the blanket she laid on in the family room was scooped up and put in her room. I closed the door and didn't go in for months. It was too painful. I walked by her closed door every day. I pictured the room exactly as I left it.

Her bedroom door was next to mine and it started to haunt me. I was constantly having nightmares and unable to move forward. My choice was to either let it continue to have control over me or take control over it. Going back to one of my core beliefs that I have control over my thoughts and actions, I decided to conquer the door and what lay behind it. I opened it and looked in. I just stood there and cried, remembering sitting in the rocking chair and reading to her or sitting on the floor playing with her. After opening the door for the first time, I still found it difficult to go back in. I decided to keep the door closed for a long time. Several months went by before I was able to leave the door open. I felt peace knowing she was part of the room and soon another child would live in it.

Brittany was born almost two years to the day after Courtney: August 25 for Brittany and August 9 for Courtney. It was with great joy that I was able to bring her home and give her a gift from Courtney. The gift of her room, toys, books, and blanket. The blanket was eventually passed down to Connor and then Hannah. It was with Hannah that it became so worn and ragged that it was thrown away. Keeping that blanket was one of the best things I could have done. A piece of Courtney lived with all three of my children. It brought joy to my heart. The kids never realized it, but I knew that it was something special.

CONNOR'S ROOM

Going through Connor's things was so different. He was twenty-four when he passed and lived in a house with some friends. Connor lived a simple life. He did not have a lot of possessions nor did he want them. The last time we talked, it was just a few days before he passed and two and a half weeks before Christmas. When I asked him what he wanted, he told me he didn't need anything. He just wanted my support and love. I told him, "I always support you. I love you." I knew better though, and there were a few things he could use. His comforter was from his youth and was torn and ragged. The next day, I bought him a comforter set, new sheets, and pillowcases. I never had a chance to give them to him.

Sometime between the day of his passing and his memorial service a week later, the girls and I along with my brother went to the house to clean out his room. The timing is all a blur. I wanted to get through it as quickly as possible. I thought the faster it was completed, the less painful it would be. I was also thinking about his roommates. I knew they would want to rent out the room as quickly as possible. They told me I didn't have to do it then. There was no rush. However, it was something I felt I needed to do. It was the right time. I wanted to get it done.

When we got to the house, there was a candle burning on his headboard. I walked in and blew it out. I didn't want to start a fire. His roommate came in and told me he lit it and according to Catholicism, it was supposed to stay lit until his funeral. Boy, did I feel terrible. I felt like I insulted him and his religious practices. I apologized. We then turned to the task of sorting his room out.

It was important that the girls and I cleaned out his room together. We did this as a family. It helped to process his passing. It gave us the opportunity to grieve together and talk about Connor. This was emotional and difficult to do. He lived in that room. He was an adult and I no longer knew everything about him. His roommates shared stories with us. I loved hearing things they did together. They told us how much he meant to them. How much they loved him. This validated what I knew all along. Connor is a kind and caring man. Even in death, Connor knew how to make his mother proud.

You will know when the time is right to do this. As mentioned earlier, it took months for me to do anything with Courtney's belongings, while with Connor, it was less than a week. When you choose to do it, be prepared for the unexpected. You may feel a strong wave of grief and find it difficult to finish what you started. That is okay. There is not a timeline in which you have to make these decisions.

GIVE IT AWAY

I mentioned he didn't have a lot. He had a bed, dresser, side table, television, Xbox, skateboards, and clothes. He had two drawers full of socks though. I learned something that day. Connor would rather buy new socks than wash and match the ones he had. Connor loved tie-dye t-shirts and he had a dozen or more of them. We offered them to his roommates.

Fridays are tie-dye Friday. At Connor's memorial friends and family were invited to wear colorful clothing or tie-dye t-shirts. It couldn't have been a better way to honor him. He lived in t-shirts when he wasn't working, and the girls picked out some for themselves. The rest of his clothes and odd and ends possessions were bagged and brought to my garage. We didn't know what to do with everything. They sat in my garage for months. I had once offered to give them to someone from church, however for some reason, it never worked out.

I avoided looking at the pile of bags for the longest time. They were in my garage and so that wasn't the easiest thing to do. After the initial pass through and once the fog lifted ever so slightly, I pondered what would Connor want me to do. It came to me that his cousin would benefit from his clothes. His cousin was grateful and was honored to wear Connor's t-shirts. He went through and took what he wanted. The rest were returned to me and I thought, "Now, what?"

In the spirit of giving to others, they were included in winter care packages for the homeless. I host an annual gratitude brunch and bring together hygiene items they need. That year they had a bonus of a t-shirt from my son. I know that is what Connor would appreciate and he'd be telling me, "Good job, Mom."

Just a few months before he passed away, we went shopping and I bought him a wool overcoat. When he wore that coat with his suit and boutonniere, he was proud. He walked taller. He was more confident. He was handsome. It is not just the coat that is special. It is the memory of that day together. We had fun shopping together. We created memories. I still see him trying on that coat and saying "Yes, this is the one, Mom."

When he moved into the house, he brought a dining room table, entertainment center and china hutch. They were pieces from my mom that he inherited. I don't think Connor ever bought any furniture. He lived off hand-me-downs. He wasn't into possessions. He was into experiences.

We left all the furniture in the house. Honestly, I didn't have a need for it, and I knew his friends could use them. I was happy to help them out. I think about his friends and the house often and know that a piece of Connor is with them.

The girls and I kept a few special things. Each of them a t-shirt or two, the skateboards, and the hockey sticks. I have his dress coat, a pair of shoes, dress shirt tie, and pants. Everything but the coat is in a box on a shelf in my closet. I don't know if I will ever do anything with them, yet I'm holding onto them. I don't have to decide what to do with them today or tomorrow as a matter of fact. I see it and look at it. The clear container lets me see what is in it without opening it. One of his class pictures is propped up and I look at it. Some days it gives me peace, others, I need to divert my eyes because it hurts so darn bad.

Taking care of Courtney and Connor's things were totally different experiences in keeping them and passing them onto family or sharing with others in need. It has been much more difficult for me to part with Connor's things than with Courtney's. I've had a tough time pinpointing why. Maybe the difference is that I knew that there would be more children after Courtney. Maybe it is because Connor lived twenty-four years and Courtney not even one year. I never celebrated a full year with her. Although I love her, we have a short history together, limited memories. Connor and I had much longer with a wealth of memories. However, sometimes there is not an answer to why the big gap. I finally gave up on trying to answer why it is so dissimilar.

The important thing is that I did it on my time. I did it when it was right for me. How I did it was the way I wanted. It gave me joy knowing others were benefiting from Connor. They may not know the significance of the t-shirt. I hope that they feel a presence, Connor's presence, and that they are loved. Connor would like that.

DONNA'S STORY

I met with Donna over Zoom. She was struggling with the tragic death of her son, and even more so with what to do with her son's belongings. We spent quite some time talking about her son, what she had done already with his room and his belongings.

After our time together, she wanted to think about her next step. After a few days, this is what she wrote, "I almost feel I want to give them to a foster child who doesn't have much. Tom would have liked that I think." I asked her how she felt about it. Her response was that she would be happy knowing Tom would appreciate it. She has donated them to a foster family. The family is excited to receive such a precious gift.

BABY LAND

Courtney is buried in what I call "Baby Land" at the cemetery. It is an area that is dedicated to children. As I walk the rows of headstones, I cry for the other families because I know their pain. The headstone tells the story of their ages. Some are obviously newborn, others a few months, and some a few years. I wonder if it was an accident like Courtney or if they got sick. I feel the parents' pain. I pray for the families. For those who passed a long time ago, I wonder how their families are doing. I don't visit the cemetery often. I don't make a special trip. It is when I am driving by and feel drawn to stop. Being there is now a healing place. I tend to her headstone and straighten up a few around hers. I find that I don't need to visit the cemetery to remember her. I remember her in different places and different times. Walking in Baby Land helps me to not feel alone. There are other mothers whose children have parted. They also suffer pain, loss, and grief. We are in this together, though never have we met. When I pray for the families, it is my hope their hearts are healing, they have found joy, and have been able to move through their loss. It brings good memories to visit and I hope that whatever you create for a memorial does the same for you.

FUNERAL ARRANGEMENTS

As a parent, you never expect to outlive your child and don't even think about burial plans in the event it does happen. Most of the arrangements for Courtney's funeral were done by her dad. Because she was only nine months old, a funeral home came forward and donated her casket and cemetery plot. We didn't have any immediate family members laid to rest, so we accepted their generosity. It made it easy. I was gripped by grief. Jesse planned most of her service. I picked the music. My cousins played the piano and sang "Jesus Loves Me." That song hits me in the heart every time I hear it.

From the day Courtney died to her funeral was a mere

thirty-six hours. She passed on a Wednesday and her service was on Friday. The coming weekend was not only a holiday but also my wedding anniversary. We decided not to taint our wedding anniversary with a burial, so it was quick. I felt this was the right thing to do, making the best decision possible in a no-win situation.

Connor and I never talked about funeral arrangements. It never occurred to us. Would he like to be buried or cremated? Without him to express his wishes, we decided to have him cremated. It felt like it is the way he would want things to be handled. Jesse planned Courtney's funeral. I wanted to make the decisions for Connor's memorial service. He is my son, and no one was going to get in the way of my decisions. Brittany and I decided that his memorial would be a celebration of life. We would bring together his friends and family to say goodbye. The question came up again, "What would Connor like?" Well that was easy. He loved Taco Tuesday, mac and cheese, and tie-dye t-shirts. It was settled.

We wanted to have his service outdoors at one of his favorite places, Daniels Park. That would have been ideal. However, the weather in Colorado on a December day is unpredictable. Once it was decided that outdoors wouldn't work, we chose to have his service at the church I was attending. I am so grateful that we did. I am grateful because the more than 300 people who attended got to hear the word of God. The pastor shared that God was screaming in Connor's ear, "Don't do it. Don't end your life." The pastor wanted Connor's friends and family to know that God was not responsible for Connor's death. It was Connor's free will and his decision.

I am grateful because it turned out to be a beautiful day. I am grateful because I got Connor into a church one more time. I am grateful because it gives me peace. I am grateful because I believe it was what Connor would have liked.

Crematoriums have played a role with Penny, Mom and Dad, and now with Connor. There are so many options now what to do with the ashes. If you don't purchase an urn, your loved one's remains are given to you in a plastic bag inside a small nondescript black plastic box. It is up to the family as to what you want to do with them. Mom and Dad were scattered at the same place, a river close to where they lived for many, many years. Penny's husband still has hers. We needed to decide what to do with Connor's ashes.

CREATING A MEMORIAL

One of the options is something called a "Living Urn," This is a package that includes topsoil, bark chips, and a sapling tree of your choice. When the sapling is planted, the ashes are placed in the hole to help feed the tree and as a final resting place for your loved one. Connor loved the outdoors, hiking, and skateboarding. We were excited about the idea of the living urn. We ordered it but waited on getting the tree until the weather was right to plant a sapling.

However, we have run into several obstacles with a sapling. I live in a condo and don't have anywhere to plant a tree. A trailhead in the mountains makes sense, however we don't get to the mountains often enough to take care of a newly planted tree. We asked ourselves, who would water it? Who would make sure a deer doesn't eat it? Who would keep it from being dug up? Not only that but digging on national forest land is illegal. Something that wouldn't bother Connor, but it does bother me. The idea of planting at a trailhead has been dismissed. This has been tough. I don't give up easily though. Sometimes answers aren't revealed immediately.

As mentioned earlier, Connor loved to skateboard and started at an early age. The next obvious place to lay his ashes and plant a tree is at the park he grew up in. Rules,

rules, and more rules. The city park won't allow us to plant a sapling. The good news is that we can have a full size tree planted in his honor. It can't be a sapling. We can't plant it. They need to. It can't be planted just anywhere. We can help decide where. We will work together to make this happen.

Get it done to have a place to remember your child. Get it done to process. Get it done and have a dedication with friends. I encourage you to take action. Don't allow creating a memorial to add to your pain. It is meant to be a place of healing.

Spring is coming and it is time. Getting the girls together to look at options has been a challenge. I want to do it myself but know that this part is not just about me. It is about them. As I write this, I am hoping that we will be deciding in the next few weeks. This is an important step for me. Not only is it a place that I can visit Connor but it is a way to give back to the community. In the years to come, the tree will grow and provide shade. Many, many years down the road, it will fall and the full circle of life will have been played out.

Grief is not to be done in isolation. Including the girls in the planning and decisions has been an important piece of their grief whether they know it or not. I've been gently guiding Hannah to participate in the process. She is feeling included, reaching out, and expressing her thoughts. Together we are healing. Grief can tear a family apart and I am determined that is not going to happen to us. I am the momma bear and will do everything to come together to support one another, love one another, and not feel alone.

Courtney is buried in a cemetery. Connor's ashes will be spread outdoors at a skate park. Why are they so dramatically different? Time. Values. Forethought. Twenty-eight years between the passing of Courtney and Connor is a long time. A lot has changed in that time. Like my values on death and dying. I've thought about how I want to be remembered.

Without specific instructions on how to take care of my son, I did what I thought was best. I did what I thought he would like.

OTHER WAYS TO REMEMBER YOUR CHILD

You may find comfort in so many other options. I've seen memorials at the place of their child's passing, maybe on the side of the road. Just like the rules at the skatepark, there are rules to roadside memorials. Be sure to check with your local department of traffic and safety.

You may find it helpful to have pictures of your child on a table or nightstand. I've seen pillows made from articles of clothing. You may want to create a photo album that you can come back to time and time again. I have Courtney's album and the many I made when Connor was a child. These albums are ones I can pick up, turn the pages, and set down. In today's digital age, it is easy to create online albums and share them. Have a friend or family member help you do this. Reliving those moments makes me happy.

Another way to remember your child is to do something in your child's name, just like I did with Connor's clothes. You may start a non-profit and give back to an organization your child admired. Listening to your child's music playlist is a way to remember and connect with them. Jewelry is also a great way to remember them. Brittany has a locket filled with some of Connor's ashes. It helps her to feel connected. Hannah has a necklace with a pendant with a set of angel wings, birthstones, and some silver leaves. It hangs on a picture above her bed. He is with her at home.

I received the same necklace as Hannah except that is has the extra words "mom" and "family." When I took my road trip, I wore the necklace everywhere I went. I went for hikes and visited churches. Connor went with me. I took the necklace off and took pictures of it on a tree, next to the water, or with a sunset in the background. He even went to church and saw the cross. It was my way of taking him and showing him places he had never been. I had sorrow and joy at the same time. Confusing, yes. Healing, yes. There is no right or wrong. Just moving forward. That is the goal. Move forward.

Whatever memorial you chose, it may initially be painful to look at. As you look at it and remember the good things about your child, the pain can lessen. It is about making a choice of whether it continues to break your heart or bring you joy. We are not meant to be stuck in grief. There are so many ways to remember and honor your child. Pick what feels right for you. Pick what gives you joy. Pick what gives you peace. This is a conscious decision. Remember I said at the start of our journey it is all about choices?

9

COPING WITH HOLIDAYS, BIRTHDAYS, AND "FIRSTS"

THE FIRST CHRISTMAS

Connor ended his life on December 14, 2018. That date, so darn close to Christmas made it difficult to even think about any sort of celebration. In my haze of grief and desperation and wanting to protect my girls, I tried to make Christmas normal. We did the usual thing. The kids were here for our traditional breakfast of homemade Swedish Tea Rings and orange juice. We had drawn names at Thanksgiving, and we adjusted the list without Connor. Even when we draw names, I get each one of the kids something. Remember the comforter I bought for Connor? Well, I returned it. I couldn't keep it. It was too painful to have in the house. It was a solemn day for sure. We made the best of what we could. It was as if all of us were in a twilight zone. All of us were dazed and shocked.

I had seen something on Facebook about a white envelope. It was placed in the Christmas tree and was the last present opened. It was a gift to the grieving family in memory of a loved one. Something they would have appreciated. I decided that would be the thing to do in Connor's honor. I donated money to Sam, who took in Connor's dog, Mac. Connor planned for Mac to be taken care of if anything ever happened to him. Mac was his pride and joy and I wanted to help get him established into his new home. I thought the white envelope in the tree would become a tradition, in Connor's memory. I wanted to make sure he was remembered. What I didn't think about then was the message I was sending to my girls. Looking back, I was starting to idolize Connor. I wanted to create everything in his honor. I was missing the opportunity to live in the land of the living.

Taking down the Christmas decorations was something I just wanted to be done with. I asked a friend to help me. It was difficult to say the least. There was a sense of urgency to get it done. There are ornaments with his picture and ones that reminded me of him. We also have a set of three miniature trees, one of which belongs to Connor. That one was even harder to put away. Through the years, it became easier to put up the ornaments for Courtney and now my wounds with Courtney were reopened. I was on a mission to start 2019 as quickly as possible. The Christmas tree from 2018 was a painful reminder. I pushed myself to exhaustion to finish taking down the decorations. I think this was a type of madness, insanity, and illogical thinking. However, it was my way of having some sort of control over my life. I couldn't control Connor's decision, but I could take charge of the decorations in my home.

MY BIRTHDAY

My birthday is on December 30. I had no idea how I was going to make it through. Again, I wanted to make things as "normal" as possible. For years, we have been celebrating my birthday at the local fondue restaurant. The girls, their boyfriends, my niece, her son, and a friend of mine went ahead for dinner. It was weird. It felt like Connor would come flying through the door at any moment. He was known for being late, especially to Christmas and dinners. It was odd. We enjoyed dinner but did not talk about Connor. I think everyone was afraid to bring him up, afraid to start crying so we avoided talking about him. I was okay with that in the moment. I believe in choices that we make. I chose to celebrate my birthday. It was not the usual level of gaiety, but it was good to be surrounded by friends and family.

It may be hard to believe that your loved one wants you to go on, live a full life. I dearly hold onto that belief and it was with that in mind that I chose to celebrate my birthday. I felt that if I had not recognized my birthday, I was setting myself up for never celebrating again. This is part of the healing process. If not now, when? When should I start moving through the process? Don't get me wrong, I was sad and just barely into the process, yet I knew in my heart that I needed to celebrate my birthday. Give yourself permission to enjoy the day, enjoy the moment.

First Christmas – Made it. Survived.

My first birthday – Made it. Survived.

HANNAH AND CONNOR'S BIRTHDAYS

Hannah's and Connor's birthdays are six days apart. Hannah is March 1 and Connor's March 7. When they were younger, I made sure they had separate birthday celebrations because I knew what it was like to combine my birthday with Christmas and New Year's. As they got older, it was harder and harder to get everyone together twice in a span of less than a week. We started celebrating their birthdays together. As a mother, I knew the pain I experienced losing a child.

The loss of a sibling is not any easier. I know the pain of losing my sister, my best friend.

However, I didn't know how to help Hannah. It was her "first." When we talked about it, she told me she doesn't measure time or life that way. Her birthday was just another year. She didn't relate it to being the first one without Connor. It made sense to me. Not everyone measures life according to Angelversaries as I do. The first year, I think we went out for dinner with her sister, boyfriend, and cousin. It was a quiet night. I did everything I could to be present and in the moment with her and not think about Connor's upcoming birthday.

For weeks before Connor's birthday, I asked myself "What do you do for a person who has passed? What do you do for their birthday?" I had been through this once before with Courtney but with Connor it is so different. With Courtney I never did anything "special" like a birthday party. Maybe it was because she never made it to the one-year mark. I never celebrated her birthday while alive so why do it in death? I struggle with why this is so different with Connor. What I decided is that it doesn't matter. I don't have to have an answer. It just is. I decided to honor my feelings and go with the flow.

I believe things happen for a reason. This is the second year without Connor. Yes, I keep track of time relative to before and after. As I write this chapter, I am between Hannah's birthday, March 1, and Connor's, March 7. It is Thursday, March 5, 2020. This would be Connor's twenty-sixth birthday. I find it difficult to even utter these words. He was twenty-four when he passed away. Time marches on and there is no stopping it.

We are celebrating Hannah's birthday on the eighth. It works out that way this year. We are having family pictures taken. Brittany, Hannah, and I. Afterward, we are going to dinner with some other family members. It is the speed that Hannah wants. She finds it difficult to celebrate only her birthday. I know she will heal and there will be a time for her to celebrate on her own. This year, Connor spoke to her on her birthday. She was in the shower and heard his voice. He told her, "Happy Birthday, Hannaher." Hannaher was his favorite nickname for her. At first this rattled her. She thought she was making things up. She wasn't though. After we talked about it, she saw it as a gift from Connor and that it is okay to be happy and celebrate.

I asked both Brittany and Hannah if either one of them were like me or felt the need to acknowledge Connor's upcoming birthday. Both replied that there is not a need to celebrate it. I felt like they didn't have the same need and desire as I did. After much prayer and consideration, I decided that was okay. They are adults and will find what works for them. It is a little bit of both worlds in the grief process. Some time as a family and some time figuring it out on your own.

CELEBRATING CONNOR

For Connor's forever twenty-fourth birthday, I decided I would do something that reminded me of him, something that we both enjoyed doing. I am going for a hike with the dogs. This lifted my spirits and I am looking forward to it. I know Connor will be with me. When I mentioned it to Hannah, she told me she was thinking about taking a hike also. Now, the both of us are going for a hike together. Brittany will be working and now that she is seven months pregnant, she won't be able to join us.

Brittany's birthday is just two weeks after Courtney's. I honestly never felt a conflict with celebrating Brittany's. It was easy. While I was married, Jesse and I acknowledged

Courtney's earthly and heavenly birthdays by mentioning them in passing. It was as casual as talking about the weather. Once we were divorced, he texted me "Always remembered. Never forgotten." Courtney was always on my mind. I didn't need a reminder.

As the day of Connor's death, also known as Angelversary, approached, I knew it would be a tough day. What do you do on that day? It is not something to celebrate. It is not something to be ignored. It is a time to be together with family. The girls and I spent the day together. In late October, I booked massages for all three of us and made a reservation for a nice lunch. We enjoyed being together. We laughed and relaxed on what could have been a highly emotional day. I think we have a new tradition. You may choose to do something entirely different. I've seen large family gatherings to celebrate a loved one or small ones heavy with grief and sadness.

I've been asking Connor's friends to send me memories of him. I am proactive about this. As weird as it sounds, there will be few people who reach out on his birthday. They have gone on with their lives. I cannot expect them to reach out to me. My inner circle will but those beyond my close friends will not. Understand this and it will keep you from being disappointed and being angry. Unmet expectations can lead to harsh feelings. Be real with yourself and those around you.

Since starting my Facebook posts, I have been blessed to meet many people. Because of my posts, a few friends were inspired to create something in memory of their child. Some have planted a garden with their child's favorite flower, placed a bench with a placard at a place they visited often, and started a garden. One that stands out is the walking path designed by Debbie T. She made a large "W" (ten feet tall by five feet wide) out of crushed gravel. She placed it in the middle of her garden. While she was making the path, she felt a sense of purpose, that she was creating a place to visit her son, a place to feel her emotions of both grief and joy. Now when she is feeling the need to be with her son, she can quietly and quickly slip out to her backyard for peace and solitude,

OTHER WAYS TO CELEBRATE YOUR CHILD

You may choose to honor your child in different ways. Some of the framework we talked about earlier is useful in celebrating your child. Look at pictures of your child. Write a love letter to your child. Write a birthday card to them. If you use social media, post about your child. Plant flowers. I've seen people pay it forward by purchasing a birthday cake for a child celebrating their birthday. You may be led to wear something that reminds you of your child. I wear tie-dye t-shirts to remind me of Connor. It is my little secret message to him that I am thinking of him.

Whatever you choose to do, I suggest you honor your feelings. It is okay to be happy. It is okay to cry. For me, it was getting through the first Christmas, first birthday, and first Angelversary. Having been through it before, I knew I would survive. I am strong. God has given me the strength.

I have reasons to live. One purpose is to be here with my family, to see grandchildren born, attend weddings, and celebrate high school and college graduations. Connor is not done on this earth. He is working through me to spread the message of hope and healing. God has His hand in this too.

> *"A man's heart plans his course, but the Lord directs his steps."*
>
> — PROVERBS 16:9 NIV

I am being led down this path to help others. We are here

to help others so they do not lose hope. My purpose is to do something useful with my hands and mind so that I may share with others in need.

There is no right or wrong way to acknowledge birthdays and holidays. A year may not seem long enough before being able to be happy and find joy again. What I do say to you is if you find yourself not being able to get out of bed, angry all the time or depressed, you may want to consider seeking professional help to process your loss. God heals all wounds. We need to be open to his healing hand though. I know it stinks. Your child is gone. Your heart aches. I've been there, done that, twice. Would your child want you to be miserable and stuck in your grief? I can venture to say they would not. Rather, they would want you to have fond memories and be able to move through this season.

Society has changed the way we mourn, how we grieve. The death of a loved one used to occur in the home and preparations for burial were made by loved ones. Since the flourishing of medical science, people are now dying in hospitals and their bodies whisked off to the morgue. Other cultures have formal mourning periods that allow loved ones to spend time together, processing the passing. Once that is complete, they can seek joy and not be judged.

I think sometimes loss travelers place expectations on themselves. They don't give themselves the opportunity to mourn and move forward. No longer are we mourning in the community, it has become a private affair. Seek your community, your tribe, in these moments.

This framework is your opportunity to get out of your head and start the path of healing. I challenge you to take a closer look at what you are doing, what you are thinking, and ask yourself if it is where you want to be. Grab this information, these tools, and put into action some of the steps to get you started.

10

SELF-CARE TAKING CARE OF OUR PHYSICAL NEEDS

We have spent a lot of time on the mental piece of processing the loss of your child. That alone will not heal you. Stress caused by grief and suffering will wreak havoc on your body if you don't do something to prevent it. While this is Chapter 10, like all the chapters, each piece of the framework can be worked out of order or done simultaneously. I encourage you to do all of them. You may focus on holidays one day, then journaling and self-care another, or do them all together.

In our grief, it is easy to stop taking care of ourselves. When we no longer give the body the care it needs, it will shut down. Grief is physical. Your heart can physically ache. You may experience extreme fatigue, restlessness, headaches, nausea, inability to eat. Grief increases inflammation throughout your body.

In Chinese medicine, grief is associated with the lungs. The lungs are responsible for breathing, which can break down in stressful times. It is not a coincidence that after a difficult period, people catch colds or get bronchitis or pneumonia. Your immune system is compromised, leaving you susceptible to illness, colds, cases of flu, and even cancer.

I am professionally trained as a personal trainer and nutrition consultant. I've seen the impact of grief on my sister and father. I mentioned in Chapter 2 that both passed away from cancer. I cannot help but see the correlation between their stress-filled lives and their diagnosis and ultimate passing from cancer.

While I can't scientifically prove that stress caused their cancer, I can scientifically prove that free radicals are caused by stress. Free radicals are extra atoms that float around in your body that are looking for a home. When they can't find a home, they damage the cells around them. Damaged cells can no longer fight off diseases such as cold, flu, and short-term fatigue. Longer-term impacts can be diabetes, heart attack, stroke, cancer, autoimmune diseases, arthritis, poor memory, wrinkles, and in extreme cases, death. These mutated cells replicate time and time again making it harder and harder to bring your body back to homeostasis or equilibrium or stability.

As a mother who has lost two children, I made my mind up that I did not want to put my remaining children through the horrifying experience of seeing me suffer through cancer. When Connor passed away, I knew I was in for a long ride of stress. Stress that, if I did not handle it properly, would have taken over my life, possibly killing me.

I am fortunate that my training and education came in handy in this stress-filled time. I was able to go on autopilot with my thinking. I knew what to do. If I was going to survive this season, I had to take care of myself.

WHAT IS SELF-CARE?

What does self-care mean? What does self-care look like? Self-care is what you do deliberately for physical, mental, and emotional well-being. We have already looked at mental and emotional and now are focusing on the physical. The physical so often is the most ignored, denied, and disregarded. However, it is an important piece in your recovery and should not be overlooked. It is part of that package of total well-being, overall health, and wellness.

As a mother, we are the caregivers. We want to take care of others. I believe the desire to nurture is inborn. We all have different levels of that nurture tendency and it makes us who we are. That nurturing instinct is also what makes our grief so deep and wide. For most of us, we spent nine months growing a developing child. Once that child is placed in our hands, they have our hearts forever. Other mothers may receive their child from another mom who couldn't raise a child. Where and how that child came into our arms doesn't matter. What is important is that we now have the child to love and take care of. They are small, fragile, and incapable of self-care. We take on that responsibility with joy and gladness, teaching them how to take care of their needs.

The first time they pick up the small piece of food and put it in their mouth we rejoice. We teach them how to eat. We teach them how to use the potty, wear a coat, and soothe themselves when hurt. Self-care is something they learn from us and we encourage them to continue to learn.

Oftentimes, we focus so much on nurturing and teaching that our health takes a back seat. It is easy to get wrapped up in the well-being of our children. When they are taken from our lives, there is a big gaping hole in our hearts. We don't know what to do or how to take care of ourselves or even why it should be done.

Taking care of your needs is not a guilty pleasure. The mixed messages we get as a mother come from within and those outside. I've seen women be judged because they take time to exercise, time for themselves, or just because of who they are. They are told they should be at home with the children. Guilt is placed on their shoulders. They fall into the trap of pleasing others and doing what others think they should be doing. If you are a mom who tells yourself that you don't have time to exercise, play, or meditate, it is time to focus on you. If you fall into either one of those lines of thinking, it is okay to take care of yourself. It is time to do what you need to do for you.

OXYGEN MASK

Put on your oxygen mask and take care of yourself. By now, you may be able to think about your purpose after losing your child. That purpose may be as simple as you wanting to live out a happy life. Maybe it is to start living and stop just existing. It may be about wanting to be present for your other children. It may be to regain the relationship with your spouse. It may be to start a movement, foundation, or nonprofit in memory of your child.

Whatever your purpose, you cannot fulfill that purpose in poor health or if you aren't around. Having a purpose makes it easier to take care of yourself. It gives focus and a desire to fight for what you want. You have made it this far, and I believe you are a fighter. You are a warrior and want to do what it takes to move forward.

Taking care of your physical needs helps you stay healthy. Taking care of your physical needs can help process your grief. Exercise, sleep, nutrition, and meditation all produce hormones that aid in digestion, healing, sleep, and stress reduction.

NUTRITION

During these stressful times after losing a child, I understand how difficult it is to eat, let alone eat well. It is easy to turn to fast food, sugary treats, and processed meals to just get by. You are not here to just get by though, are you? You picked up this book for help, for answers in getting through your grief. You decided you wanted to take care of yourself and this is a great place to be.

Even if I am eating the recommended nine to thirteen servings of fruits and vegetables, I am still not getting the nutrition my body needs. Our body needs the vitamins, minerals, and phytonutrients from the food we eat. However, the quality of our food is not what it used to be. Food develops like a baby. Babies are meant to be in utero for nine months to develop lungs, heart, limbs, brain, and so much more. When babies are premature, those organs are not fully developed. The same is true with plants. They need to finish ripening on the vine, on the tree, or the plant to have those nutrients. When they are picked early, the plants cannot finish ripening, thus missing the essential nutrition. Not only is our food picked before fully maturing, further loss of their nutritional density is made worse because it can be several weeks before it is in your kitchen and you are eating it. The moment it leaves the vine, it starts to lose the nutrition it started with. I live in Colorado and the spinach at the grocery stores comes from California. It has been in several warehouses, multiple trucks, and uncertain temperatures before being stocked on the shelves to be brought home.

I already lived a healthy lifestyle and knew that I needed to be even more proactive when it came to my health. For years I have been eating fruits and vegetables in a capsule from Juice Plus+. They are dried plant powders that have all the nutrients that we lack when we don't eat enough fruits and veggies. I am so grateful that I've been taking them for nine years. They helped boost my immune system in a time when I couldn't afford to get sick.

I was a single mom with three kids working as a personal trainer. I worked long hours. As a trainer, I only got paid when I trained a client. I was paid by the session. When I wasn't with clients, I was hustling new ones. Missing time from work would cut deeply into my finances. When I would get a bad case of bronchitis, I had to work through it. There was no missing sessions, no matter how hard I coughed, no matter how bad my ribs hurt from coughing, and no matter how bad my head hurt.

I started eating Juice Plus+ because it made sense. Getting the nutrition from thirty different fruits and veggies helped rebuild my broken immune system. It was broken because of my recent divorce and the stress caused by it. It was broken because I wasn't eating right. It was broken because I wasn't sleeping. It was broken because I wasn't exercising. It may seem odd that I was working in a gym as a personal trainer and not exercising, but I was serving others, putting myself last in line to be taken care of. It has been a lesson I've since learned about putting my oxygen mask on first. I was taking care of my kids, working crazy hours, and ignoring my needs. Those tiny little capsules saved my health. I stopped getting the nasty bronchitis, I have more energy, and enjoy a peace of mind that I am practicing self-care.

Those tiny little capsules saved my family's health as well. My youngest daughter would get strep throat three or four times per year and each bout typically took two rounds of antibiotics. That meant she was on medication for six to eight weeks every year. I knew that was not the direction I wanted to go. Now, her strep is gone and if she does get sick, it is a slight cold and she does not take antibiotics.

I know that nutrition is a huge component of prevention. If we don't give ourselves the necessary tools, then we can't fix a problem before it occurs. Think of it this way. You drive a car and a car needs gas. If you fail to fill up the tank, then you run out of the fuel that allows your car to run. You may run out of gas at any moment. Most likely it will not be convenient as you may be going to work, meeting a friend for dinner, or amidst a trip to the emergency room. Any of those scenarios would be stressful. That is why you fill your car before you run out.

That is where Juice Plus+ came in for me. It filled my immune system tank. I wanted to make sure I wasn't getting sick. It was a safety blanket around my kids. I knew it was running in the background as my insurance policy to prevent us from getting sick.

The day after Connor passed away, I doubled up on my Juice Plus+. Juice Plus+ is food. It carries a nutrition label, so taking more of it was adding the benefits of eating more fruits and veggies. I like that I cannot overdose on it. If I eat too much, the worst that can happen is needing to stay close to the restroom. Mother Nature has her way of working her magic. I double up on the nutrition I get from more fruits and veggies. Not to keep hounding on it, but Dad and Penny died from cancer. I believe I can, God willing, prevent cancer. I will continue to include Juice Plus+ because I will never know what I don't get. I may never know why I didn't catch a cold, the flu, or cancer. Prevention works in the background – we never truly know if it worked or not. All we know is that we stayed healthy.

This was all new and strange to me in the beginning. The more I learn, the more I understand how nutrition has an impact on our health, especially in a grief state.

SUGAR

Food that has sugar is addicting. It is an intense craving for more sugar. Sugar impacts your moods and energy and breaks down your immune system. Unfortunately, sugar is added to most processed foods and in moments of grief, it makes sense to reach for the easy solution. The meals brought in by caring friends and family are long gone. You may not have the energy or mental wherewithal to plan, prepare, and cook a meal. I understand.

After Courtney died, I did not want to cook. It was not a priority. However, when I found out I was pregnant with Brittany, that changed. I knew that I was responsible for a growing little person and it was no longer about just me. I made some changes. I stopped drinking soda. I didn't overdo it, but it was a place to start. I added more water and made sure I kept going to the gym. Yes, I was in the gym at nine months pregnant.

EXERCISE

But as a grieving mother, you think you don't have the energy to even get out of bed or off the couch. There is good news in the compound effect of exercise. One simple step draws your body and mind to wanting more. Start with simple and small things you can do. Take a walk around the block. Getting your body moving in small steps is a victory. I like to keep track of my progress. There are several places you can do that. Your journal that you are using is a great place to document what you are accomplishing. A calendar that hangs on the wall is another great option. This is one where you can see your activity at a glance and celebrate a string of days together. If there is a gap in activity, a calendar is a great motivator to start again. This is about progress, not perfection. If you miss a day, give yourself grace and start anew the next day.

The endorphins, epinephrine, and norepinephrine are released with exercise and help to elevate your mood. They can reduce stress and the perception of pain. If you recall, when I was working as a personal trainer, I wasn't getting my workouts in. I missed it and knew what it meant to me. My mood is better, and I sleep much more soundly when I move. I am back into the swing of it. Exercise makes a difference.

Cardiovascular work compounds. What that means is if you walk for ten minutes in the morning and ten minutes at night, that is as effective as walking twenty minutes all at one time. Do yourself a favor and get up and move for ten minutes. Do it consistently for thirty days and evaluate how you are doing. Did you find you slept better? Was your sadness lifted, even if only temporarily? You may notice your thoughts are more positive and you have a glimmer of hope.

AFFIRMATIONS AND MEDITATION

I am sure you have heard at least once in your lifetime about meditation and the benefits. You may even have heard that you need to be a monk, not speak to anyone, and isolate yourself in a jungle. While that is an option to meditate, it is not required. Meditation can be as simple as repeating a phrase or humming a tune over and over. Some sample phrases or affirmations are:

I am okay.
God loves me.
I am strong.
I am loved.
I am smart.
I am beautiful.

Affirmations are said in the present tense. Saying them in

the present tense works with the subconscious mind. When we solely rely on the conscious mind to make change, it prevents us from moving forward. It is those inner thoughts that drive our decisions, and changing those is a great place to start.

BREATHWORK

Another aspect of meditation is breathwork. There are a variety of techniques, but the basics are that you focus on breathing in and breathing out. There are different tempos, different thought processes, and connection with your inner spirit.

One of my favorites is the box technique. Think of your breathing pattern as a box. In the upper left corner draw a horizontal line to the right. This line represents your inhalation. Now draw a line straight down. This represents your exhalation. The third line goes back to the left representing your inhalation again. The next line is straight up, connecting to the original starting point. You have now created a box pattern to follow for your breathwork. With each line, or breath, count to four slowly. With the inhalation, breathe deep and push the fresh air down deep into your lungs so your belly expands. As you exhale, empty your lungs and belly. Repeat the box breathing five to ten times. Clear your mind of everything but the effort it takes to follow the box.

Breathing like this slows down your heart rate, clears your thoughts, and allows space to think. The quietness allows you to hear God. It is here that you will hear His answers to prayer.

SLEEP HYGIENE

I mention sleep hygiene and most people look at me like I am crazy. This is a relatively new concept. Fifty years ago, we did not have the technology we have today. Television sets were being introduced to the home, but they stayed in the family room for family viewing and family time. Somehow, they moved into the bedroom and started disrupting many things, including sleep.

Eventually other technology made its way to the bedroom including computers, cell phones, tablets, smart speakers, blue light clocks, security systems, and baby monitors.

The art of preparing oneself to go to bed and sleep has been lost. The ritual of washing one's face, brushing one's teeth, and donning sleepwear is a forgotten ritual. Instead, the TV blares nightly news of tragedy and devastation. Cell phones emit blue lights that stimulate our brains rather than allowing them to relax. Social media is a black sinkhole that draws you in and won't let you out. Add to this the fact you are already in a place of grief and unrest; it is no wonder you have difficulty sleeping. Brain fog, forgetfulness, and impaired judgment are all signs of sleep deprivation. You may also notice weight gain, poor digestion, and diminished motor skills.

Improving your sleep hygiene is an important piece of self-care. Serotonin, the sleep hormone, increases with the more sleep you get. Getting quality sleep is a major step in helping your body to heal. It is during sleep that your physical body heals, and your brain relaxes. It is also one of the easiest forms of self-care, if you decide to do it.

Remove the TV from your bedroom. The bedroom is a place for rest and relaxation not disaster stories or nasty political campaigns. The last things that you hear before going to sleep are what are on your subconscious mind, and negative thoughts are not what you want to feed your brain. Remove other electronics as well: laptop, tablet, and cell phone. If you are using electronics as your alarm, buy an old-fashioned alarm clock. As for baby monitors, as a mother your senses are already heightened and you will hear a child. Remember that nurturing feeling? It goes a long way. Security systems can be seen from other locations besides your bedroom. These suggestions may be a challenge for you.

Again, start with something small, remember why you want to improve your sleep, and be deliberate in your actions. Getting sleep can be easier said than done. A few things that I do when I can't sleep are meditate, focus on sleep hygiene, read, journal, and pray.

HYDRATION

Dehydration is a special danger for bereaved parents because the shock of their losses often leaves them stunned, powerless to focus on their needs, and without the energy to carry out any plans. You may also experience general lack of energy, loss of motivation, general aches and pains, or headaches. Our bodies are 80 percent water and when we don't replenish what we use, our organs can shut down. We need water to detoxify our bodies and flush out the toxins that accumulate. During stress, we produce extra toxins that can stay in our system. The only way to get rid of them is to drink water. And I mean water. Coffee, tea, sodas, or alcohol do not replace water.

It is recommended to drink at least half of your body weight in ounces of water. For example if you are a 120-pound woman, then you need to drink at least sixty ounces of water. You will see your skin replenish, energy improve, and digestion start to move. Give your body the water it needs.

JULIE'S STORY

Julie is one of my former personal training clients. We lost touch over the years. Recently she was led to reach out to me. Initially it was for no other reason except to touch base during the pandemic we were in. She told me her nephew took his life. She was close to him and was having a hard time with her loss. She was surprised to learn about Connor. It now made sense why she called me. It was not a coincidence and we were meant to chat.

We talked about her nephew, what she liked to do when they were together, and what he was passionate about. She was grateful that I was available to listen, understand her journey, and bear witness to her loss. We transitioned to talking about her health.

During our training together, I taught her the value of taking care of herself. She knew in theory what to do but had fallen off the path. Work had taken over, family obligations increased, and complacency set in. She was no longer taking care of herself.

When I asked her to recall how she felt when she was exercising, getting sleep, eating well, and drinking water, her eyes lit up and a wide smile crossed her face. She told me she felt great. Her attitude was one of gratitude and she was sleeping well. Oh, yes, those are the positive benefits of taking care of yourself when times are good. I asked her if she thought this would apply in her current situation. She pondered for a moment and replied, "Yes, of course it does." She was correct. All we needed to do was reestablish those routines. We agreed that I would be her accountability partner for the next thirty days. She would text me at the end of each day what she accomplished. Did she exercise? Did she eat well? Did she get the required sleep? Did she drink enough water? Did she complete her meditations?

After those thirty days, Julie was well on the path of consistency in taking care of herself. Not only was she better equipped to process her nephew's passing, she was now in a place she was able to share her transformation with her nephews mother, Gloria. Gloria saw there is hope to find joy and we are now working together to help her get there.

Taking better care of yourself can also be one of the paths of personal growth. We spent a fair amount of time talking in Chapter 10 about the options. Remember, one simple change creates a snowball effect on your health. The need to focus on becoming healthier can be immediate. It changes how you think and feel about your body. How much abuse can it withstand before breaking down? Without your health, you can't help someone else. Consider exercise, sleep, water, and nutrition paths to make a positive change in your loss journey.

These are suggestions. There is no right or wrong. Do what feels right for you. Take what you like and leave the rest, but do take something. You are here for a reason. You want to move forward in your grief journey. Self-care is an integral part of that journey.

11

CAN GRIEF BE AN IMPETUS TO PERSONAL GROWTH?

WHAT IS PERSONAL GROWTH?

By now, you may be thinking I am insane to even suggest you consider doing anything besides crawling under your bedcovers and staying there. The cavern of heartache and pain is real. How can I ask you to peek out from under the covers and think about personal growth? What is personal growth anyhow? Why should you care?

Personal growth means improving your behavior and habits, and refers to techniques for building positive habits, behavior, actions, and reactions. However, the growth after the loss of a child takes it a step further. Growth is positive change that an individual experiences as a result of the struggle with a traumatic event. The loss of a child is a traumatic event.

Why would you want to be open to a positive change in your life? Experiencing the loss of a child can leave you feeling angry, depressed, lonely and a host of other emotions. In your grief journey, you may continually focus on the tragedy which limits your possibility of moving forward. You can stay trapped in your grief and find yourself lost, isolated, and deeply depressed. Or you can find hope, peace, and joy. You have no choice about grief, but we do have choices in grief – to grow up or to grow down.

PERSONAL GROWTH

Personal growth is found in multiple places, different modalities. It comes from formal classes or life experiences. I've mentioned several types of personal growth already in this book, but I wanted to go a little deeper. I never knew the personal growth I have been doing for a lifetime would help me in one of the darkest of darkest seasons. Personal growth past, present, and future is another piece on the framework for recovery.

Over the years I have participated in some level of personal growth whether it is reading a book, taking a class, or working with a coach. I've always felt I could benefit from learning something about myself or new ways of doing things. I learned this from my dad who taught me an insatiable desire for learning. I often refer to myself as a professional lifelong learner. If I could take classes and never have to put into practice what I learned, I would be okay with that. But we both know that doesn't work. We need to take what we learn and practice it to make ourselves a little bit better every day. When we do, we make progress in our grief.

When the kids were young, the four of us took karate lessons together. As part of the training, we were responsible for reading numerous leadership books – two of them were *7 Habits of Highly Effective People* by Stephen Covey and *It Worked for Me: In Life and Leadership* by Colin Powell. All these were meant to guide and teach the kids leadership, kindness, and gentleness. The kids were five, eight, and ten, which is quite young to read and comprehend the content of these books. As the faithful parent, I was the one who read them, absorbing what they said. I soon learned to take these books to heart for myself and grow as a parent. A family is a tribe and needs strong leadership. The same skills of leadership applied as a fitness manager, leading a team of twenty personal trainers.

I have a small army that is available for me at any time. However, in my time of loss, it is still important that I apply the skills of leadership to my relationships. Writing notes, telling others how much I care, and acknowledging them deepens our relationships. They know I couldn't do it without them, and this all came from books I read seventeen years ago. I call those lessons from the archives to use them now.

GROW WITH GOD

Developing or deepening your relationship with God is an avenue of personal growth. I decided to learn more about God. What does He desire? He wants us to surrender to Him, love Him, and give our troubles to Him. We do that through prayer, meditation, and studying the Bible.

For the past year, I have been following a program to read the Bible in one year. I journal about what I read and my interpretation and ask God to teach me throughout the day what He wants me to learn from that scripture. Am I supposed to share the gospel or show a kind gesture or offer words of wisdom? This new level of spirituality has challenged me in ways I never thought I would consider. The results though are that I am growing in a way that God wants me to. I have taken the focus off me and now have something positive to look to. He guides me in daily activities, decisions, and thoughts.

WRITE A BOOK

I decided to try something totally new which has taken my comfort level off the charts. I wrote this book you are reading right now. Until now, I did not consider myself an author. Writing was not high on my skill set. I did not know how to write a book. I knew I couldn't do it on my own. I needed guidance. I decided to get help. I had some self-doubts, a lot of negative self-talk. Who was I to write a book? Ultimately, I overcame the obstacles because the result is greater than the challenges. I did it. I reached out because I knew that I had something valuable to share with others. I knew that my experience could help somebody, somehow. I felt if I kept this information, I would be denying others the possibility to heal. This took me out of my grief and grew up, rather than down.

Through personal growth, I found value in who I am. I discovered that others need me. I trusted that God wanted me to do something big. Writing a book may not be what you are supposed to do. The cool thing here is that you get to choose what you want to do. You may have a desire that has been dormant for years to learn something new. Now may be the right time to try it. You may have seen something on TV, in the movies, or on social media that you want to give a go. It doesn't have to be as big as writing a book or jumping out of an airplane, it can be simple and small like trying a new style of cuisine at a new restaurant. As the Nike commercial says, "Just do it."

APPRECIATION FOR LIFE

Other ways that I have seen a positive change is the way I appreciate life. Worrying about the "stuff" is no longer important. The stuff is the latest smartphone, current year car, fashion clothes, or the hottest watch. You know what your stuff is.

Life is too short. Live in the moment. Stop and smell the roses. All true statements. Things we might consider even more now that our children are gone. Our hearts are so deeply wounded because of the moments we will never experience with our children. It could be their first steps, high school graduation, college commencements, weddings, grandchildren, and of course all the holidays and birthdays.

What is crucial is relationships with friends and family. I know that I say "I love you" to family even more than ever. I prefer experiences together instead of giving material objects. For my kids' birthdays, they choose what restaurant to eat at and what activity they would like to do. Connor loved the Waffle House. Even though it wasn't a restaurant I liked, the family went for his breakfast. I couldn't believe what he ordered. It was called "A Heart Attack Waiting to Happen." I vividly remember that huge plate with eggs, waffles, chili fries, and cheese. No wonder it was called that. I also remember watching him eat it, not believing he ate the entire thing, and the fun we had together celebrating his special day.

Connor and I shared a daily business mentoring tip and would chat about what we learned and express how we would use it in our lives that day. Those daily tips are about being better, maybe just a little better, every day. I still receive those tips and think about Connor when I watch the videos. I concentrate on how I can help someone else. It is a simple thought that can create change in the right direction.

Volunteering and serving others are ways to expand beyond ourselves. One of my mentors sums this up beautifully: "When you are having a bad day, take a moment to make someone else's." Look for opportunities to help another. Make a conscious decision to open the door, smile, say hello, let someone in line, forgive another driver's road rage, or buy someone else's coffee. These are impromptu day-to-day things that you can do.

In addition to small daily acts of service, I love to plan larger events and give back. I host an annual gratitude brunch. Brunch started out as just that, brunch. I wanted to bring my friends together and celebrate our friendships – new and old alike. From brunch, the event morphed into assembling winter care packages for the homeless. We collect donations for essential items and put them in bags to give the homeless as we cross paths in our day-to-day activities.

I must say that was difficult the year after Connor passed away. Hosting an event like this takes planning, coordinating efforts, and time. I felt like I was in a fog and didn't know what I was doing. By using the framework mentioned in this book, I pulled off a successful event. What charitable organization is on your heart that you would like to give back to? It could be one that your child would appreciate you donating your time to in their memory. Your child is looking down on you and saying, "Way to go. Thanks for doing this." Helping others is so impactful and positive. It helps those who you serve while at the same time your body produces feel-good endorphins that elevate your mood and reduce depression and anxiety.

Courtney lived to be a rousing nine months, was just beginning to crawl and smiled when I called her name. "Courtney, Momma loves you." She grinned from ear to ear. She was the first of the three children I longed for. I went on to have Brittany and Connor. My original plan was complete – or was it? I had three children. Never thought I would have to consider three children living or not. I never considered Brittany or Connor to be rainbow children. This was a term I wasn't familiar with until someone brought it up. I had to look it up. Here is the definition from Wikipedia, "A rainbow baby is a term for a child born to a couple who have previously lost a child due to miscarriage, stillbirth or death during infancy. These subsequent pregnancies can bring 'strong feelings of anxiety, guilt, and even fear' but also 'immense joy, reflection, healing, and mixed emotions.'"

I decided to have another to complete my dream of three living children and was blessed with Hannah Green. All I have ever received from her coming into my life is joy. There is no question that she is meant to be here. She is a gift from God. I am incredibly grateful for her.

If Courtney had not passed – giving way to new life – I would not have Hannah. You see, I got more than I ever imagined. Blessed to have four children enter my life. Would I change anything? Having Courtney and not Hannah? Definitely not.

As for Connor – he has given me new beginnings: that three-week road trip to find myself and my strength to become who I am meant to be. The me who comes out of this will be stronger, self-confident, and courageous.

SCOTT'S STORY

During crisis, people either put their head in the sand or rise above it. I prefer to look for the positive. Through a recent conversation, I helped my friend Scott move from seeing only the negative to seeing the positive. This was not an easy transition. He knew something wasn't right about his attitude. He had the feeling he was pushing friends away and didn't know why. He came to me because he was feeling lonely.

Scott's daughter passed away two years ago. We had wonderful conversation about his daughter. She was so kind and loving. She had gotten that from him, but now since she was gone, he wasn't like that. He was negative, pushed friends and family away, and was not happy.

I told him I understood all of it. It is not easy to be positive when your child is gone. He agreed and with a barely audible voice, asked, "How do I get back to who I was?" My heart went out to him because I've seen the pain before of being lost, not being the person you were before the loss of your child, and totally confused as what to do next.

We spent some time talking about who he was before. We looked at what inspired him. He wrote a list of the things he wanted to do. He told me the values he lived for. He shared his "before" dreams.

Next we discussed how he would live up to those values, be inspired, and how he would fulfill those dreams. Scott wrote five positive affirmations about himself that he read three times per day. He started paying attention to the words he heard from those he admired. He listened for the positive in what they said. He then implemented those thoughts into his conversations. Within a week, he saw a shift in the way he spoke and felt about himself. He felt good about what he was saying and ultimately he was reconnecting with those he alienated. Scott found that small steps in personal growth were huge in appreciation for life. We are now ready to move forward and explore his belief in God.

Personal growth is just that. You decide what area in your life you would like to expand in. Do you have a hobby you would like to learn? Is there an organization you can volunteer in on behalf of your child? You have options. It may take several attempts until you find one that helps. You can make a list of the areas you want to grow in, master the activity, mark it off, then move onto the next item. Personal growth takes the focus off your grief and channels your energy toward positive outcomes.

12

YOU CAN DO IT

GRIEF JOURNEY

This grief journey that you are on is not a one-and-done type of thing. It has impacted you for now and forever. It is called a journey for a reason. A journey is traveling from one place to another, usually taking a long time. To recover and heal from the loss of a child is an unending journey. The trials and tribulations you encounter may lessen.

However, you will still find events, locations, sounds, and people that trigger your pain. Those triggers can come running at you from nowhere and surprise you that they are even occurring. It could be something that gnaws on you for quite some time until it comes to a rapid boil. You don't know how to prepare for it. Your instinct tells you there is something wrong. You are uneasy, but you just can't put your finger on it.

Then it occurs to you that one of those special days is approaching. The ones that you wish never happened. The ones that you wish your loved one could be with you for. The one that you wish you could have just one more of. You may feel like you are back to square one. This is normal. Two steps forward. One step backward. Be patient with yourself.

THE FRAMEWORK FOR REGAINING JOY

The framework that we built together is a starting point in your journey. It is a new chapter in your life. The tools we have gathered here and shared are available for you from now until eternity. While all this seems so simple and straightforward, you will run into obstacles. Some of them will be easier than others to overcome. Some you may be able to sidestep and put off until a later date. However, if you want to move forward in your loss journey, it will be necessary to slay them, defeat them, and put them to rest. For each one of the frameworks I've listed some obstacles I encountered and others that I anticipate you could run into.

FRAMEWORK NUMBER ONE: JOURNAL

Remember that you started off with writing down your thoughts? Even though I mentioned it is the easiest place to start, just getting started can be difficult. Your thoughts, doubts, and questions can be saboteurs. You may ask "Does this work? How does this apply to me?" You may start and stop multiple times. Your family may not understand your need to journal and may make fun of you. As your grief sets in, you may feel overwhelmed. You might even misplace your journal or feel it takes too much time. You may not feel it is a priority. I had a few of these things happen to me, yet I know that when I journal, it makes all the difference in my day.

FRAMEWORK NUMBER TWO: FIND YOUR TRIBE

You may feel totally alone on your journey. It is true what people say: Until you have experienced the loss of a child, you will never understand what it is like to grieve for them.

Reaching out to others is not normally what mothers do. We are supposed to be the strong ones, the ones who support others. I find that rather than reaching out for help, mothers will try to resolve problems by themselves. Important questions to ask yourself are: How is that working? Are you seeing progress? Is this how your child would like to see you?

It can be confusing as to who your tribe is and where to find them. Remember, finding your support network is extremely important. You may need assistance in identifying your inner circle. Don't be afraid to reach out for help

FRAMEWORK NUMBER THREE: TALK ABOUT YOUR CHILD

Even though you want to talk about your child, you may encounter resistance in doing so. Those closest to you may not want to talk about them. They may pass your desire off as excessive and obsessive. They may tell you that you should "be over it" by now and move on. They don't understand your grieving heart and place a low priority on this important topic. Or, much to your surprise, someone who barely knew your child is shouting to the rooftops about their grief causing you to become agitated. You may feel cheated and want to retreat because no one understands you. These are common but I believe you will learn how to talk about your child and feel good about it.

FRAMEWORK NUMBER FOUR: FIND YOUR HIGHER POWER

If you have not explored a relationship with God, this can be a controversial subject. Non-believers will do everything in their power to dissuade you from learning more. They will tell you lies; they will call you names and judge every action you make. They may also have you question where was God when your child passed? You may think that God is supposed to make life easy and He wouldn't be putting you through this difficult time. You may question if God is real or if the Bible is factual. Believe me, God is with you at all times. God will protect you from those who are against you. Be open to learning more and how God will ease your pain and suffering.

FRAMEWORK NUMBER FIVE: REMEMBERING YOUR CHILD

I've seen disagreements over how to remember a child. One parent wants one thing and the other parent wants another. A division occurs and the memory of the child is tainted with discord within the family. In addition to relationships, families may be facing financial struggles to create the memorial they want. Location and type of memorial have also been an obstacle within families. Where you want to erect a memorial may not be allowed. Getting family to agree on timing of the dedication can be problematic. It is times like these that, instead of fighting, families need to come together.

FRAMEWORK NUMBER SIX: DEALING WITH HOLIDAYS, BIRTHDAYS, AND FIRSTS

I believe this is one of the hardest things to do. It is so much about your mindset. If you do not have a plan or mentally prepare yourself for these days, they will be as bad as the day your child passed. The thing about holidays and birthdays is that they happen every year, every 365 days. There is no avoiding the date. You may question how you will make it through the "firsts," but what happens on the second, third, fourth and so on? How will you prepare for the rest of your life knowing these days will come time and time again? You may react to others in ways that you never did before and create animosity because of it. Grief may show up at the least convenient moments.

FRAMEWORK NUMBER SEVEN: SELF-CARE

To think about taking care of yourself without guilt is huge. You may be the biggest obstacle to taking care of yourself. You may think it costs too much money. You may feel that you don't know you enough. You doubt it can help you. You may also be judged for being selfish. People who tell you those things are not those you want to be part of your tribe. It may be a challenge to find those who encourage you to practice self-care.

FRAMEWORK NUMBER EIGHT: PERSONAL GROWTH

Personal growth can scare the people around you. They may discourage you from becoming a better person. They like you as you are even if you want to improve. They may question why you want to do so because of their insecurities of losing you as you grow and change.

As for yourself, you may possibly deny the opportunity to grow. Maybe you tried before and gave up before seeing results. Being prideful may stop you from seeing that personal growth can help with your grief. One of the largest obstacles is negative self-talk and not believing that you can do something like this.

WHY YOU ARE HERE

You are here because you lost a child. I am sorry that you are going through this. You are reading this book because you want help. You want help to make it through a difficult time in your life. This book and its framework are the support you didn't know you needed but were looking for. Their purpose is to help you navigate your loss journey, to support you in your desire to heal. It is my dream that you found the framework helpful as a fellow loss traveler. We are on this journey together. If you found this to be impactful, please do not keep it to yourself. Please, please share it with a friend or family member who would benefit from learning these tools.

Grief is a continuous journey. It is a long and winding road. There will be ups and downs. Some days will be better than others. It gets better. I know. I understand. I've walked in your shoes. However, it does not get better by itself. You will need to use the tools that I've given you. In the beginning, it may feel awkward or like they are not working. Keep practicing. This is about progress and not perfection.

The tools will help. Use them often and where needed. They will come in handy when the difficult situations occur. They will help you when you anticipate grief sneaking up on you. They will help you feel like you can handle any situation that arises.

13

CONCLUSION

HELP IN MOVING FORWARD

This is a journey I not once in my wildest of dreams thought I would be on. I never considered myself to be strong, a Wonder Woman, or inspirational. I now know that I am that and so much more. I am faithful to God. I am a better person because of my loss. I am an empath. I have courage to do the things I never thought I could. I am a leader. I am smart. I am loved. I have something to share with others. I am gifted. Above all else, I am a mother who still loves my children.

I made it. I look forward to a bright future. I am grateful for the time I had with Courtney and Connor. Radical acceptance was my first step in both losses. With Courtney, I didn't have tools or resources to tap into. When I was able to come out of my daze with Connor's death, I looked around to figure out how I was going to make it through child loss number two. It was evaluating life lessons and the things I have done that brought me to the conclusion that God has given me all the tools necessary to make it through this season.

I am blessed with everything I have experienced and brought together. I would not wish my lessons on anyone else. I would not wish to take on someone else's lessons either. They are meant for us as individuals.

Losing Courtney, making it through a divorce from an alcoholic, finding my faith in God, having two children go through twelve-step recovery programs, discovering my love of learning, working with a business coach, nurturing a strong tribe and circle of friends, having a family that I love, running and operating my health and wellness franchise – all of these experiences were necessary for me to step into my purpose. It is both the good and bad that taught me the lessons I needed to learn to survive Connor's death. It is what brought me to you. You have reached the end of the book and now have the framework for moving through the loss of your child.

Journaling helps to clear your head, take away confusion, and express your emotions in a safe, non-judgmental place. It is an easy thing to do. All that is required is paper and pen. Keep doing it. It is a lifelong tool for you.

Your family may or may not be your tribe or support system. They fumble for words or don't say anything for fear of saying the wrong thing. Until they have walked in your shoes, they do not understand the tears, the heartache, and the yearning for your child. It is important to intentionally seek out support as you walk this loss journey.

Teach others how important it is to talk about your child. As a mother, you want to talk about your child. Others are waiting for permission from you to speak their name. Give them permission. Tell them you would like their name to be spoken and memories shared.

Finding your higher power, or God in my situation, can be

totally daunting and confusing. How do you find someone to answer your questions? What does belief in God look like? I know that as a "rookie" Christian I had no idea what I needed to learn or what to do. I started attending church on a regular basis. I joined a Bible study group. We focused on learning the word together.

Coping with the holidays and special days are a process. Find what works for you. It may take several years to decide. Are you going to uphold the traditions from when your child was with you? Are you going to start new ones? Or will it be a combination of new and old? I found that a combination is what worked for me. Remember, you have the freedom to change your mind and find what works for you.

When the time is right to give away, clean out, or dispose of your child's belongings, consider what your child would want. Can you make a difference in another family's life by helping them out? I also suggest keeping some items that are special to you, that make your heart smile and bring back good memories.

Are you taking care of yourself? It is easy to push down and ignore your basic physical needs. Exercise, sleep, hydration, and nutrition are what sustain your body. They are the foundation upon which you can begin to rebuild from the impact of grief. I believe there is a place for the mental as well as the physical healing.

If it were not for Connor's passing, I would not be stretching myself by having written this book. That is huge for me. I feel God led me to this. I have taken a horrible, devastating loss and made the best of my choices in the aftermath. Your personal growth does not have to be big and scary. It can be simple and small, as long as you move forward with it. You might even struggle with what or how you would like to experience personal growth.

You, too, can be more than you ever imagined. You can be

happy again. The tools to function in your new norm are before you. Use them to face the challenges that present themselves. I understand you will have days that are tougher than others. You are strong. You will make it. You made the first step in your healing by picking up this book. That alone is an accomplishment to be proud of.

What you do with the framework is up to you. Practicing each step by yourself is an option. If you find yourself still struggling to put them into practice then maybe, just maybe, we should chat. My heart's desire is to help you to be able to move forward from the loss of your child, even be it one small step at a time. Having been through loss not once but twice, I learned a trick or two. I've shared most of what I've learned, yet am convinced there are things I have forgotten.

As a mother, the pain and heartache from losing your child can be unbearable. You could choose to shut down and not ever look toward a positive happy future. The choice is yours. I am all about choices. I can with all my heart tell you that with some work and intentional healing, you will be able to find relief in your grief. It is time to be open to the healing powers within. You can and will do it. I believe in you.

If it were not for my life experiences, I would not have a toolbox to build this framework for surviving the loss of Connor. It does stink that I am even in this situation. My heart still aches. I've learned how to cope and manage it. I made a choice twenty-nine years ago that I would not let the passing of Courtney keep me from living a fulfilling life. I had and still have so much more to offer the world. I am not done living. Focus on the positive and be grateful for the small things. Gratitude goes a long way.

ACKNOWLEDGMENTS

This book is a result of the encouragement I received from family and friends who saw something in my journaling that I did not see. They saw inspiration and hope from my trauma and my path to recovery. Until I penned this book, I never thought of myself as an author. I am so grateful that my message is now available to everyone. My words are not mine. They are from God above and they flowed through me to my fingertips to the paper.

I am grateful to Pat Huss Sheveland who referred me to The Author Incubator. We met on Facebook after the death of my son. When I asked about who she worked with as a mentor in writing her book, she recommended The Author Incubator. Their program walked me from start to finish to complete my book that is not just informational – it is transformational. A book that truly makes a difference in many people's lives. It gave me the opportunity to share my experiences and teach others how to regain joy and enjoy time with their family after the loss of a child. Writing this book has been an exercise of itself on journaling. It has been huge in my recovery.

To The Author Incubator team: Special thanks again to Angela Lauria, CEO and Founder of The Author Incubator, for believing in me and my message. To my Developmental Editor Andrae Smith and Managing Editor Cory Hott, thanks for making the process seamless and easy. You gave me the guidance and the freedom to do what was needed.

To my inner circle who are lifelong friends who have been with me through both Courtney and Connor: Roxane A, Renee S-B, Renee S-J, Ruth B-T, and Lisa S. We have known each other for a long, long time, and I am blessed to call you friends. I love you more than you can imagine. Thank you for all you do.

Other friends that I've gained over the years through sports, work, and my children: Stacia S, Sharlee T, and Holly F. I love getting together for a glass of wine, Saturday morning Cornerstone Breakfast Club, and hiking. I look forward to those times we spend together

To my Juice Plus+ Family, near and far: Jan S, Gail S-M, Jess G, Bob S, Jennifer M, and Sean M. You believe in my ability to help others. You mentored me, stood by me, and taught me more than you will ever know. My Venus Vixens: Kathy P, Lisa C, Diana B, and Lori W-U. I love seeing your beautiful faces on Zoom every week for the past three years. My Brave Leaders Pod: Holly W, Jennifer W, Julie C, Pam A, and Tammy E. You made it possible to be vulnerable and write my story.

I say thank you to the Juice Plus+ Company for their mission: "to inspire healthy living around the world and build a stable and lasting company that will help as many people realize their dreams." There are so many others who touched me that I can't thank everyone. It just proves that we leave a stamp wherever we go. Please keep leaving that positive impact.

To my family on earth and in the heavens. My brother Phil

who supports me when I call. He always has words of wisdom. Fred, my brother-in-law who challenges my way of thinking. I love when we get together. My cousins on my mom's side, the "official" blood ones and the "adopted" ones alike. We have grown closer together in the past few years and I am so excited to be part of your lives as well as you are part of mine. The heavenly family is Courtney, Connor, Mom, Dad, and Penny, all who left an indelible imprint on me. Thank you for all the great memories. I realize that you are looking down on me and telling me to press on. Thank you for your signs from Heaven. I know you are with me.

Finally, to my family that I am so proud to be the matriarch of. My daughters Brittany and Hannah, my niece Mickey, nephew Thaide, and soon-to-be-born grandson. Blood is thicker than water and we stick together. I am looking forward to a long healthy life with you. We have so much to give to the world. Thank you for putting up with me and loving me.

ABOUT THE AUTHOR

Peggy Green is a health and wellness enthusiast who helps mothers process the loss of a child so they can enjoy time with family and find happiness. After the loss of her second child, she discovered that she was meant to help others through grief. Peggy started as a grief coach, utilizing the tools and resources she gained during a lifetime of overcoming adversity, trauma, and loss. Peggy is a mother of four children, two in heaven and two grown girls.

Peggy brings together her degrees in business marketing and exercise science to help her clients gain insight into behavior that impacts their health.

Along with her degrees, she obtained a certification as a

wellness coach and multiple personal trainer certifications from the American College of Sports Medicine and National Academy of Sports Medicine. She practiced as a wellness coach and personal trainer for twelve years. She guided clients to sustainable lifestyle changes in the areas of quitting smoking, sleep patterns, exercise, nutrition, and conscious and subconscious thinking. She now develops customized plans to set individuals up for success, both one-on-one and in small groups.

Peggy is a Colorado native who loves the outdoors, and currently lives in Highlands Ranch, Colorado. During the warm weather, you may find her hiking, running, camping, playing pickleball, or romping with her dogs. Family is a top priority, along with her relationship with God. She has donated over twelve gallons of blood – just because!

ABOUT DIFFERENCE PRESS

DIFFERENCE
PRESS

Difference Press is the exclusive publishing arm of The Author Incubator, an educational company for entrepreneurs – including life coaches, healers, consultants, and community leaders – looking for a comprehensive solution to get their books written, published, and promoted. Its founder, Dr. Angela Lauria, has been bringing to life the literary ventures of hundreds of authors-in-transformation since 1994.

A boutique-style self-publishing service for clients of The Author Incubator, Difference Press boasts a fair and easy-to-understand profit structure, low-priced author copies, and author-friendly contract terms. Most importantly, all of our #incubatedauthors maintain ownership of their copyright at all times.

LET'S START A MOVEMENT WITH YOUR MESSAGE

In a market where hundreds of thousands of books are published every year and are never heard from again, The Author Incubator is different. Not only do all Difference

Press books reach Amazon bestseller status, but all of our authors are actively changing lives and making a difference.

Since launching in 2013, we've served over 500 authors who came to us with an idea for a book and were able to write it and get it self-published in less than 6 months. In addition, more than 100 of those books were picked up by traditional publishers and are now available in bookstores. We do this by selecting the highest quality and highest potential applicants for our future programs.

Our program doesn't only teach you how to write a book – our team of coaches, developmental editors, copy editors, art directors, and marketing experts incubate you from having a book idea to being a published, bestselling author, ensuring that the book you create can actually make a difference in the world. Then we give you the training you need to use your book to make the difference in the world, or to create a business out of serving your readers.

ARE YOU READY TO MAKE A DIFFERENCE?

You've seen other people make a difference with a book. Now it's your turn. If you are ready to stop watching and start taking action, go to http://theauthorincubator.com/apply/.

"Yes, I'm ready!"

OTHER BOOKS BY DIFFERENCE PRESS

Stop the Weight Gain Cycle: 7 Steps to Getting Healthy after Gastric Surgery by Daye Ambersley

Breakup to Breakthrough: 10 Steps to a Spiritually Enlightened Life after Divorce by Lana Gajic, B.Sc, M.C.

Storytelling as a Therapy Tool: Using Story to Heal Trauma and Abuse by Heidi Henyon

Love the Job, Lose the Stress: Be a Badass Band Director without Burning Out by Lesley Moffat

Reinventing Yourself: The Guide to Navigate Life Transitions and Resilience after a Traumatic Event by Rita Sampaio, PhD

Know How to Help Your Loved One with Cancer: The Whole-Hearted Support Guide by Jelena Spasovski

Heal Your Neck Issues and Let Your Throat Chakra Shine: The Spiritual Guide to Moving Forward Pain-Free by Cheryl Stelte

If I'm So Spiritual, Why Am I Still So Anxious?: The Soul Seeker's Guide to Reclaim Your Joy by Joy Stone

Live Well beyond Breast Cancer: How to Get through Treatment and Back to a Life You Love by Birgitte L. Wilms

THANK YOU

Congratulations on finishing *Life after Child Loss*. I am so proud of you for taking steps to learn how to cope and find joy after losing your child. This is not an easy journey, but I hope you now know you can enjoy your family and be happy again.

Visit https://youtu.be/9NPRsDAIkMU for a free self-assessment to determine where you are in your loss journey.

I stand beside you and am passionate about helping other moms move through the loss of their children. Let's walk together. Let's grow together. Let's thrive together.